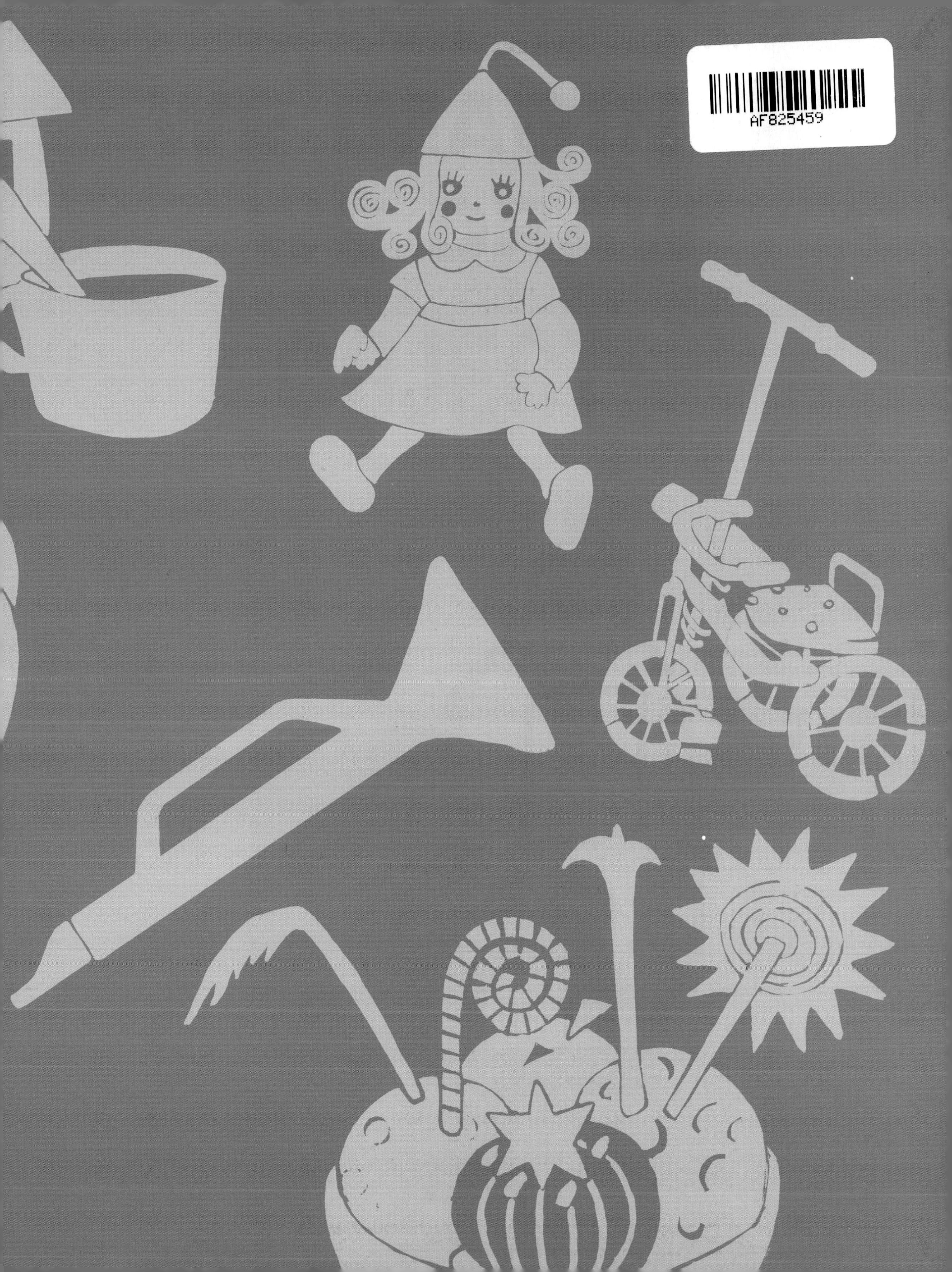

The words in *italic type* are explained in the Glossary on page 48.

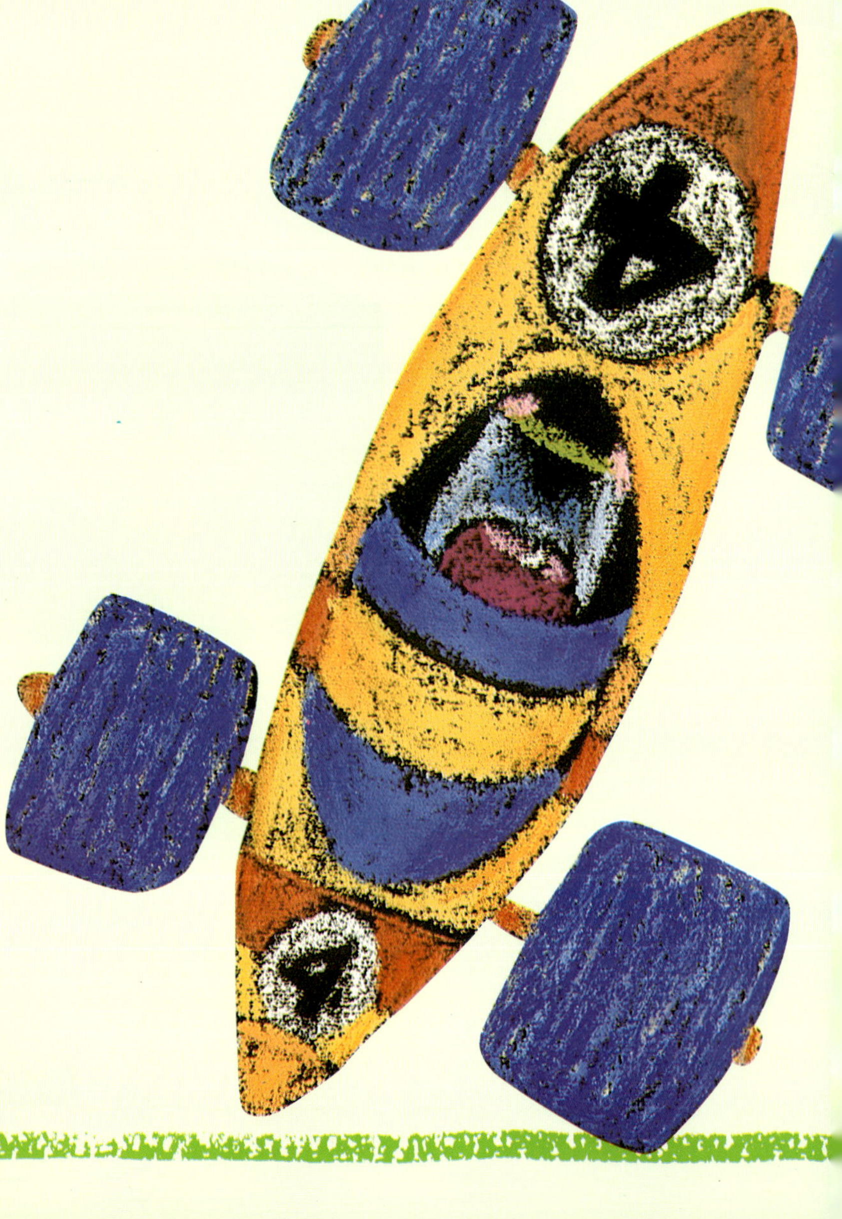

Original title of the book in Spanish: *Dibujar y Crear Objetos*

Published by Parramón Ediciones, S.A., Barcelona, Spain.
Author: Parramón's Editorial Team
Illustrators: Parramón's Editorial Team
Translated from the Spanish by Edith V. Wilson

All inquiries should be addressed to:
Barron's Educational Series, Inc.
250 Wireless Boulevard
Hauppauge, New York 11788

International Standard Book No. 0-7641-5042-1

Library of Congress Catalog Card No. 97-21413

Library of Congress Cataloging-in-Publication Data
Dibujar y crear. Objetos. English
We imagine, we draw. Objects / [author, Parramón's Editorial Team ; illustrators, Parramón's Editorial Team].
p. cm.
Summary: Provides instructions for various drawing projects, including a dining room collage and a beach scene on wood.
ISBN 0-7641-5042-1
1. Drawing—Themes, motives—Juvenile literature.
2. Drawing—Technique—Juvenile literature. [1. Drawing—Technique.] I. Parramón Ediciones. Editorial Team.
II. Title.
NC730.D5213 1997 97-21413
743—dc21 CIP
AC

Printed in Spain
9 8 7 6 5 4 3 2 1

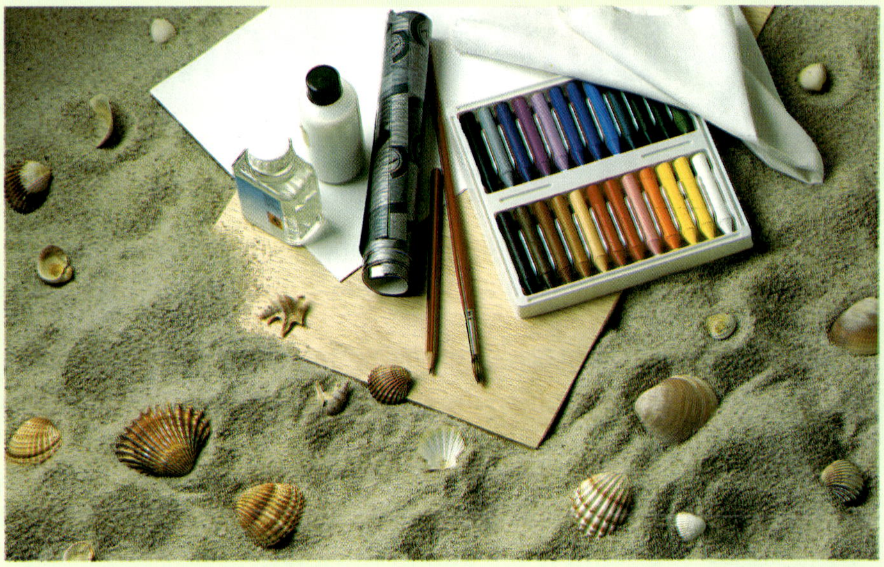

Contents

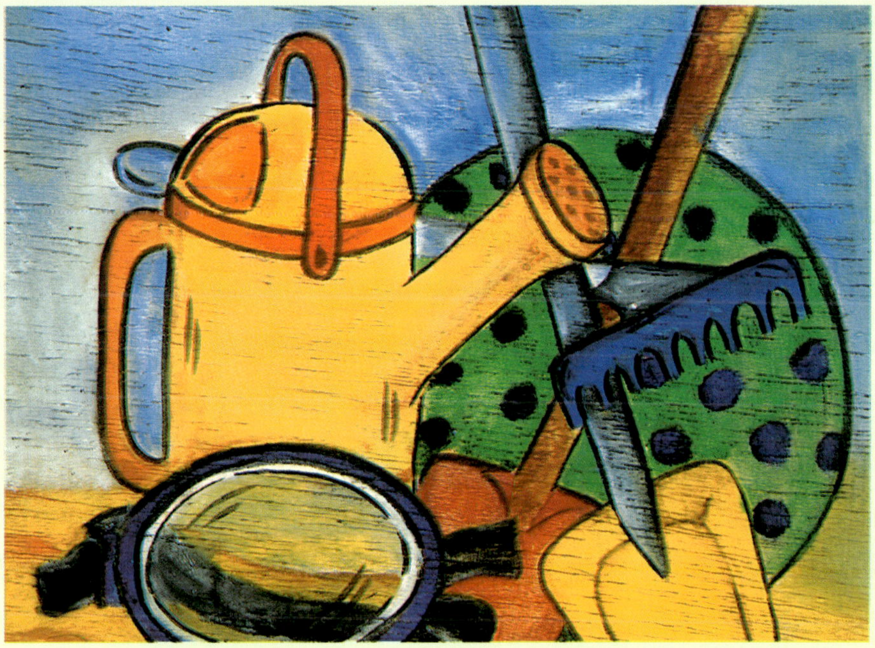

A Formula 1 Racer on Sandpaper

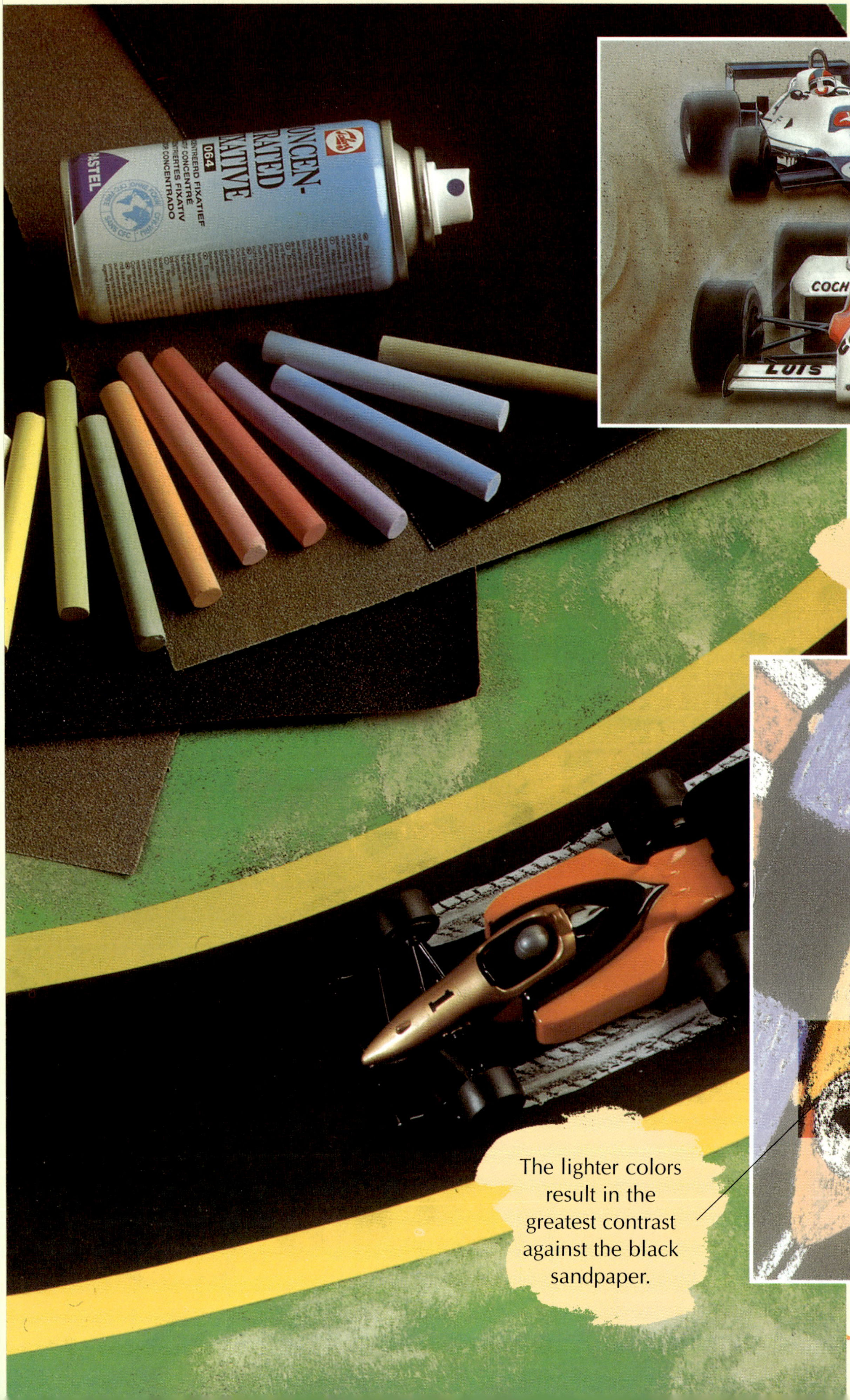

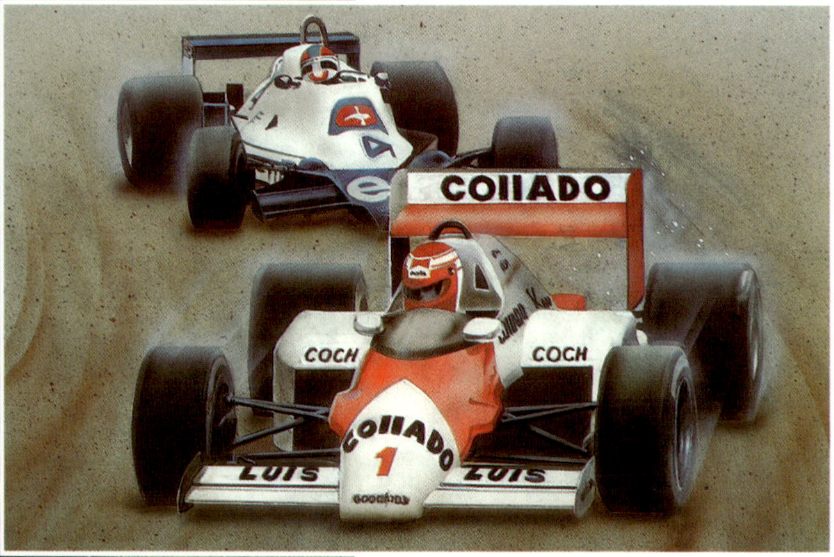

Leave a fine line between colors. The sandpaper's black color will serve to separate them.

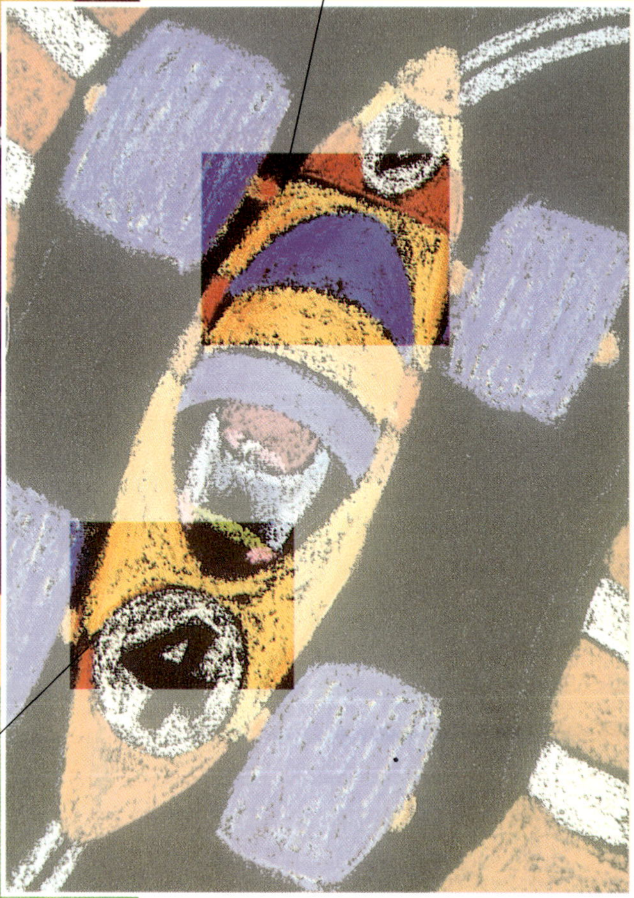

The lighter colors result in the greatest contrast against the black sandpaper.

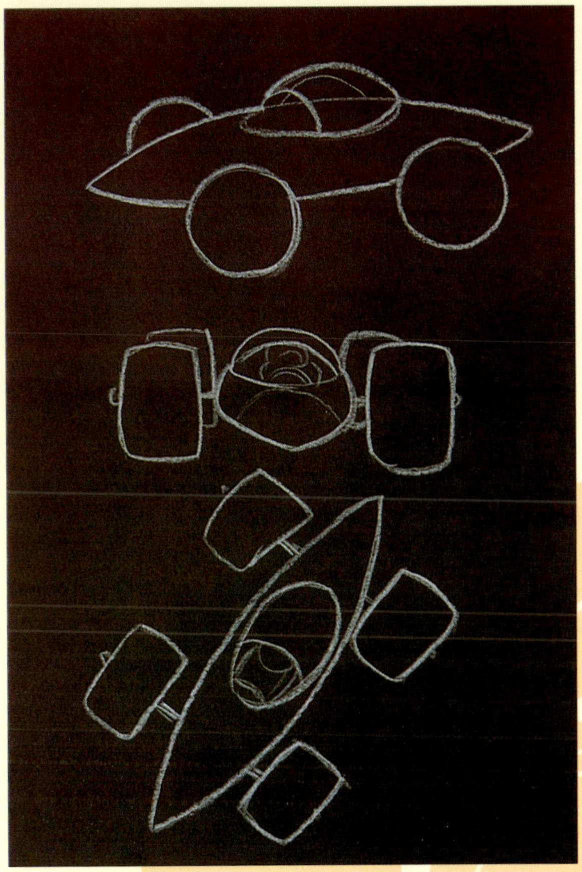

1 Begin with a *sketch*. Here, we have drawn a racing car. We tried different angles: side, front, and aerial views.

2 You'll be using a piece of black sandpaper for this work.

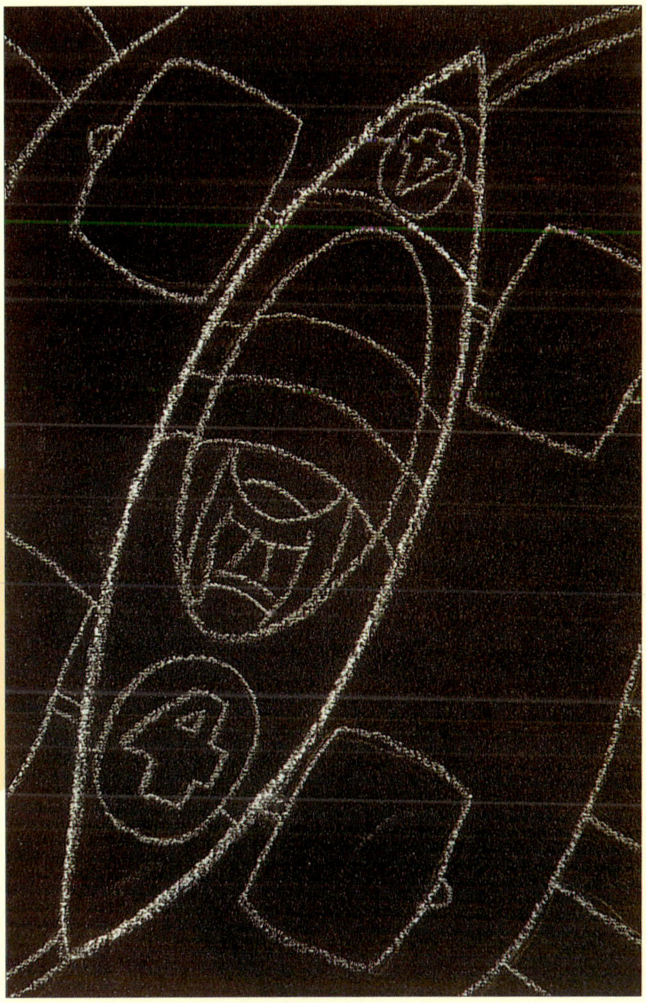

3 Compose your drawing using white chalk.

Useful Tips

You can experiment with sandpaper of different grades and various *tones* of tan. The coarser the sandpaper is, the more *texture* it will give you in the final results.

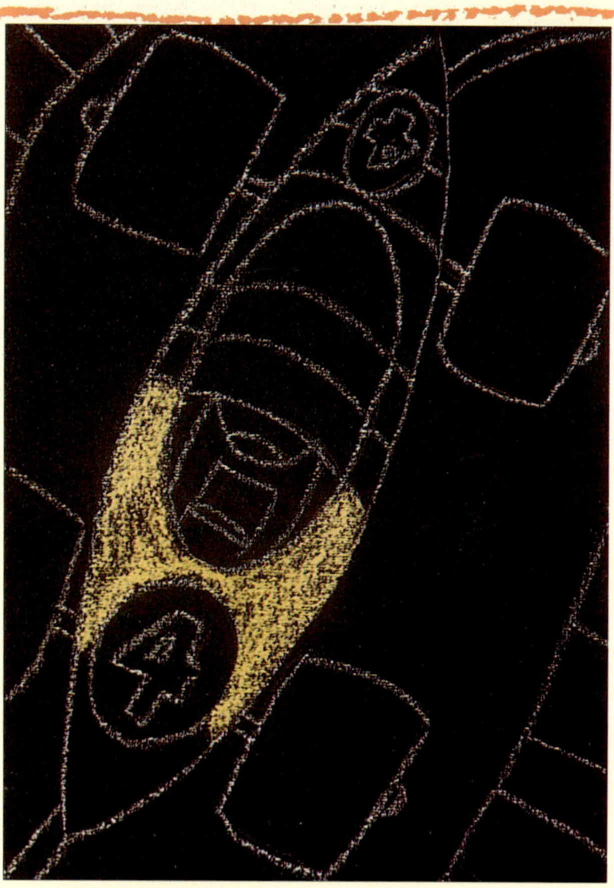

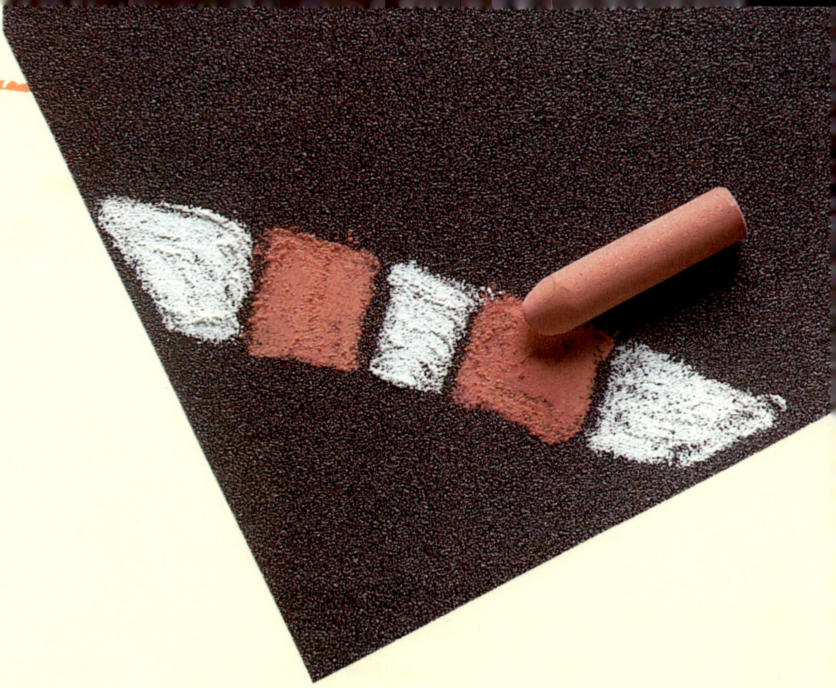

4 Add the details with chalks of different colors.

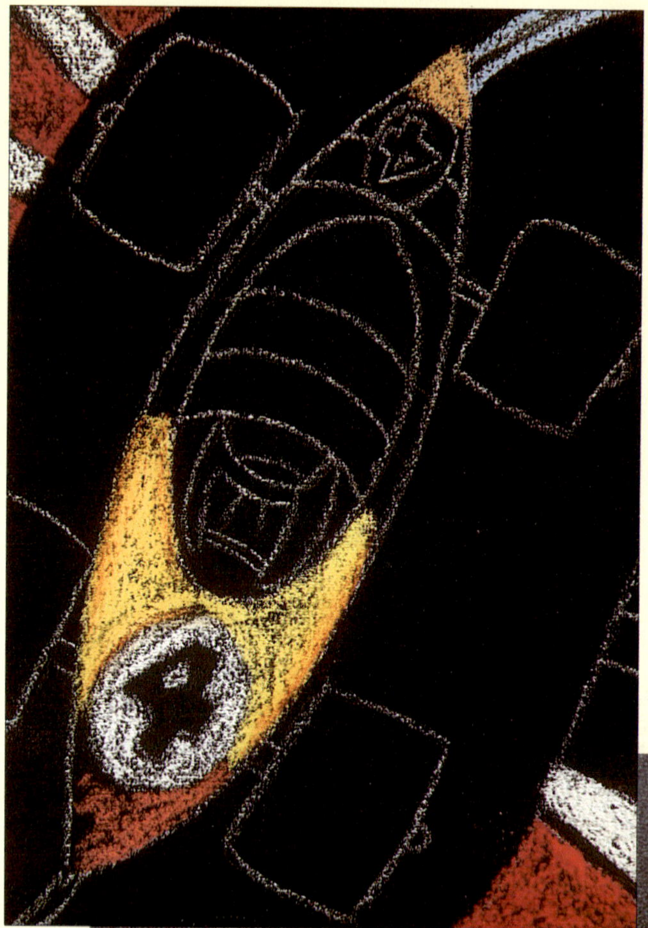

5 To make an object seem three dimensional (or solid), use colors from the same range and of different tones—for example, light and dark yellow and orange. Apply the lighter color first. Then, go over the *shadow areas* with the darker one.

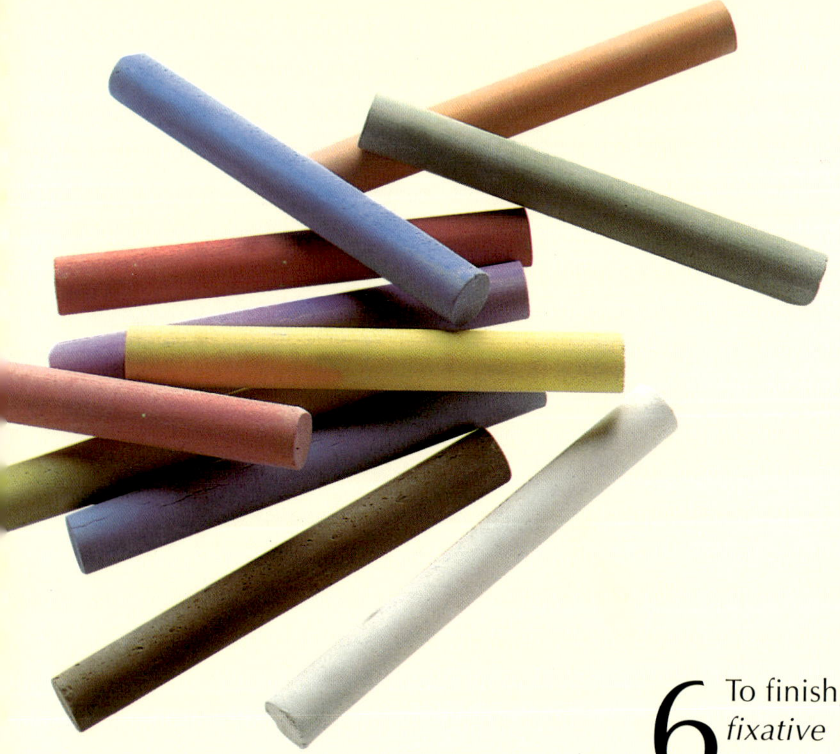

6 To finish, apply a coat of *fixative* or, if you have none, use hair spray applied lightly.

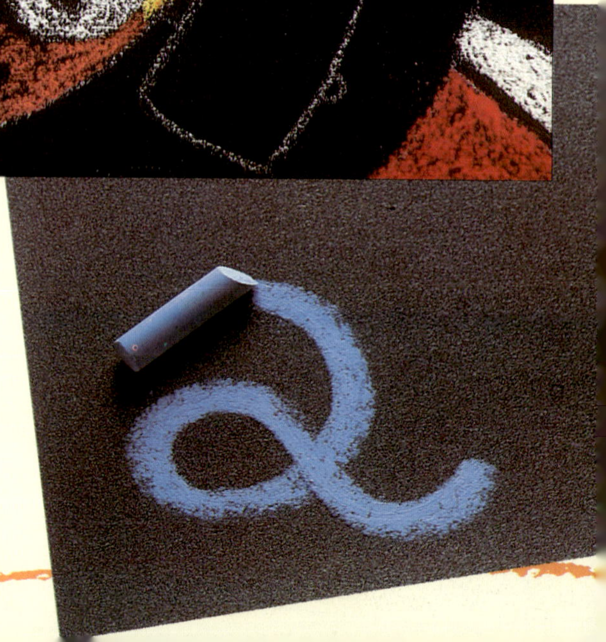

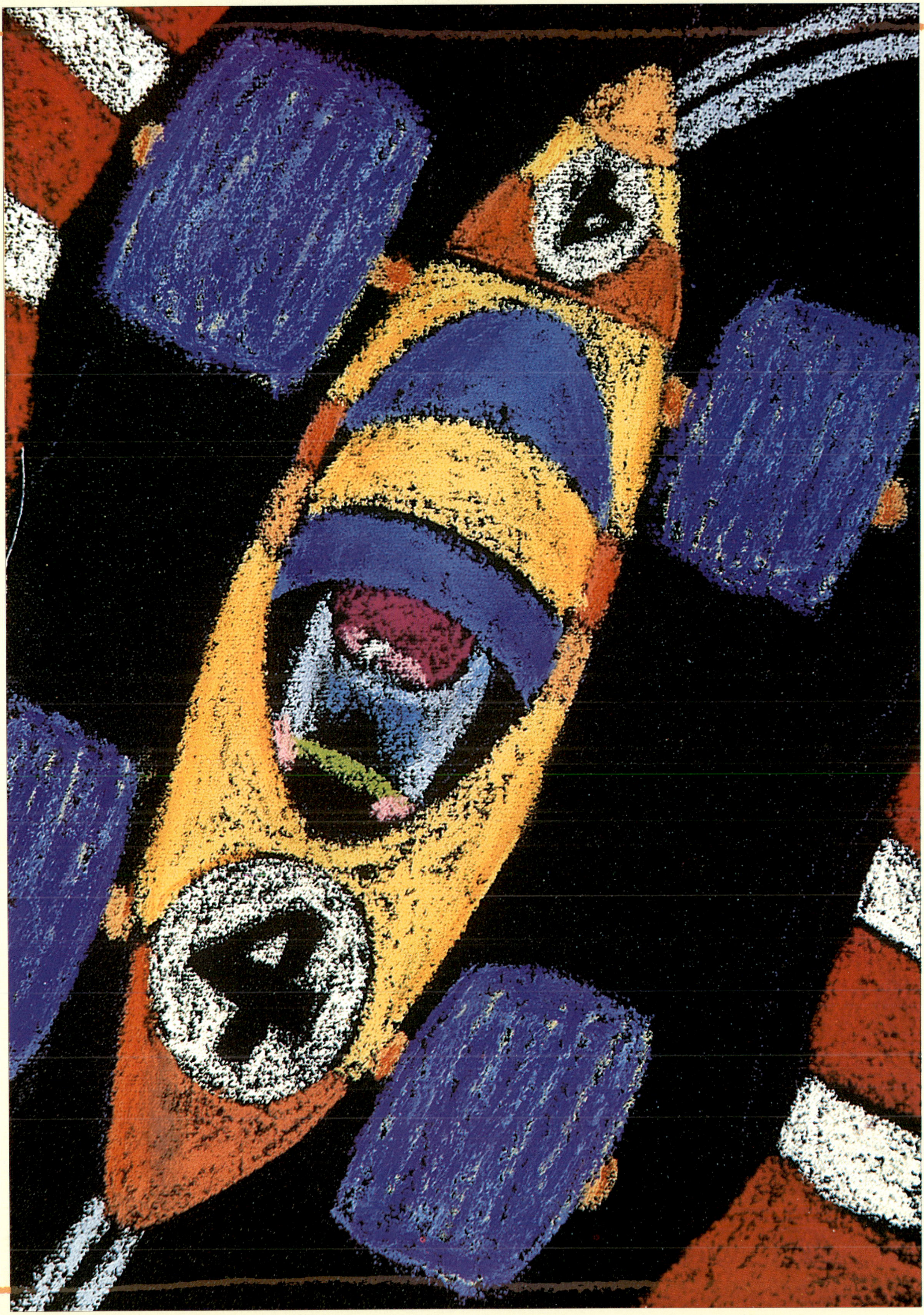

Shading Desk Objects with Marker Pens

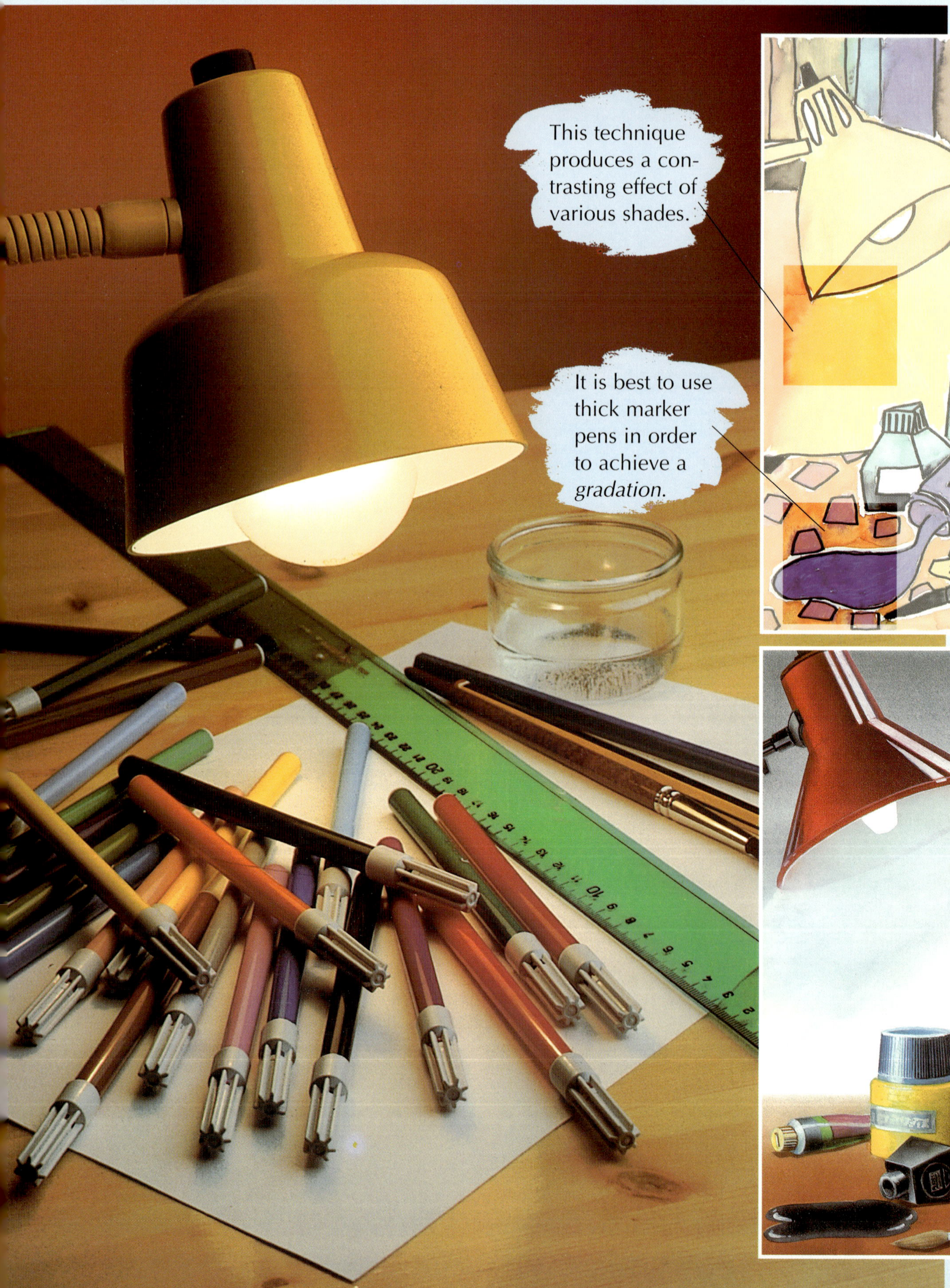

This technique produces a contrasting effect of various shades.

It is best to use thick marker pens in order to achieve a *gradation*.

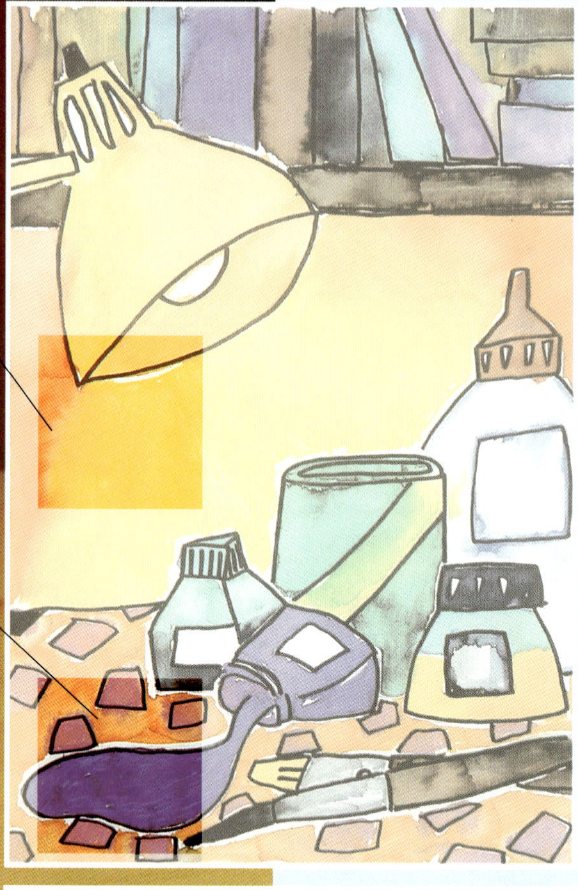

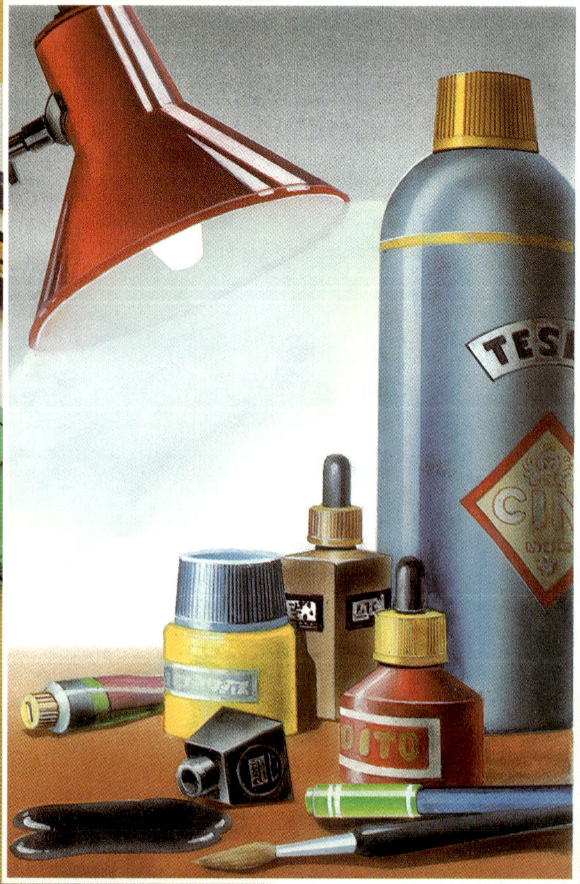

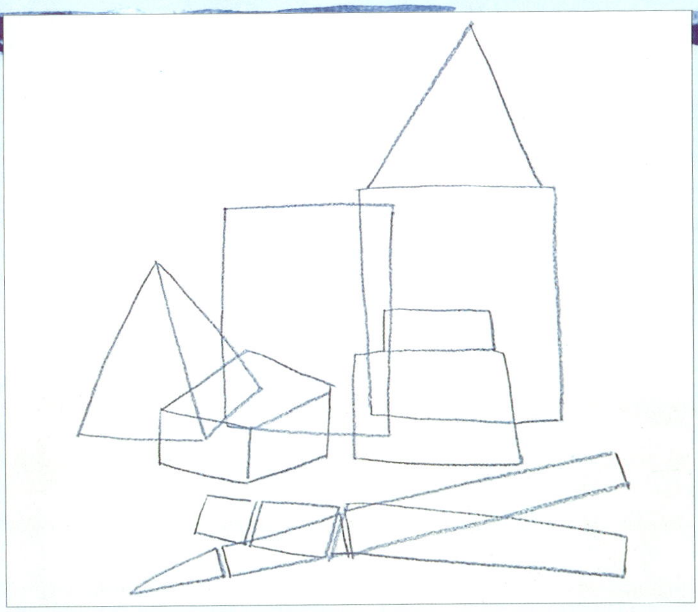

1 Prepare your form sketch.

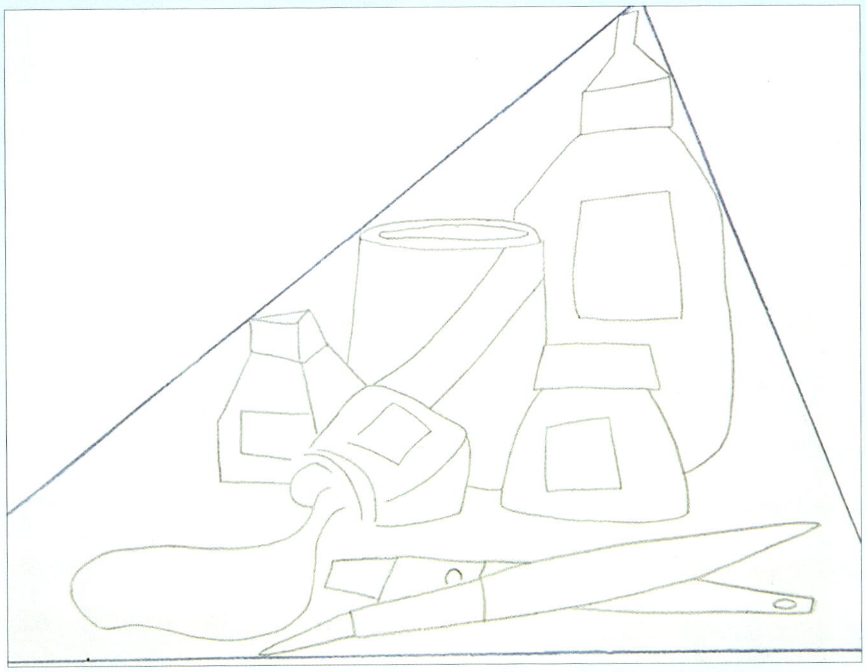

2 Draw and format your composition. In this case, the arrangement is based on a triangle.

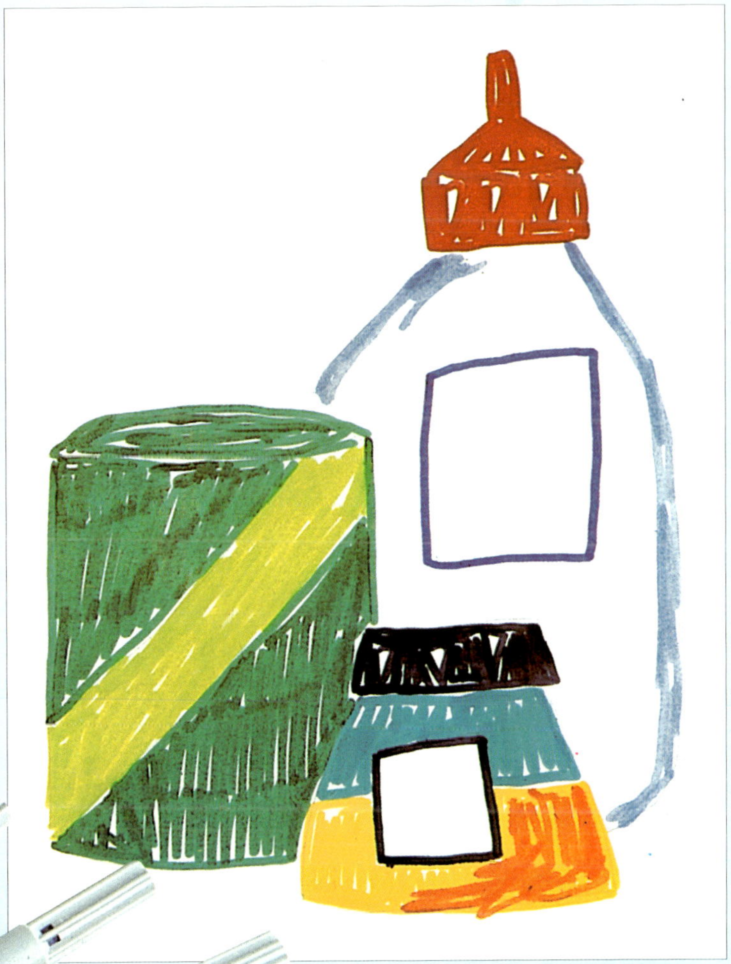

Useful Tips

Marker pen inks that are not water based can be thinned and spread on the paper with a little alcohol. Ask an adult to give you some in a small bottle with a tight cap.

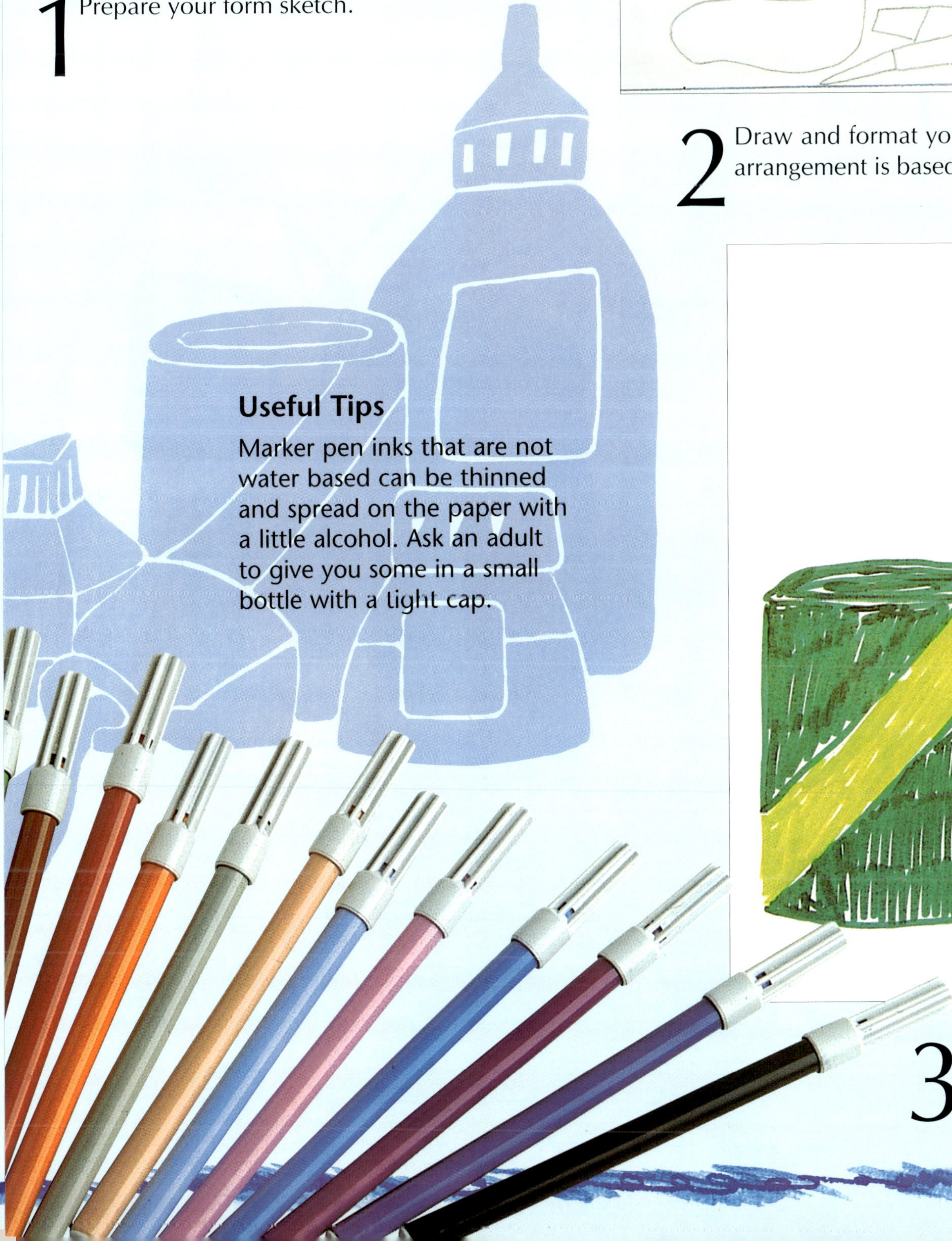

3 When painting with markers, the dark tones are used over the light ones to obtain a gradation.

A Beach Scene on Wood

When working on a dark back-ground, the light shades appear brighter in color.

Use a small amount of turpentine to achieve a paler color.

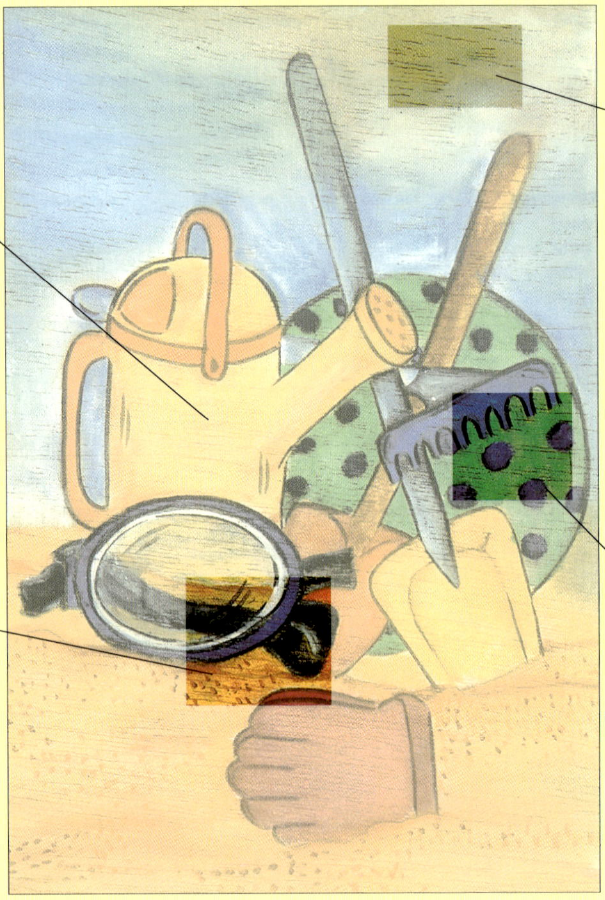

Ask an adult to give you some *gum turpentine* in a small bottle with a tight cap. Dampen a crayon with a few drops of turpentine.

Apply the crayon directly to the wood. The grain of the wood will show through the color.

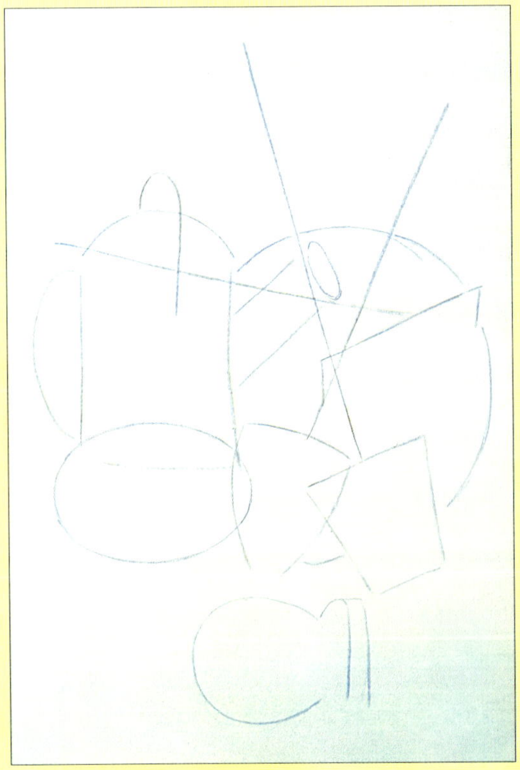

1 Make a form sketch of each object to find its proper *proportion*.

2 Sketch the composition.

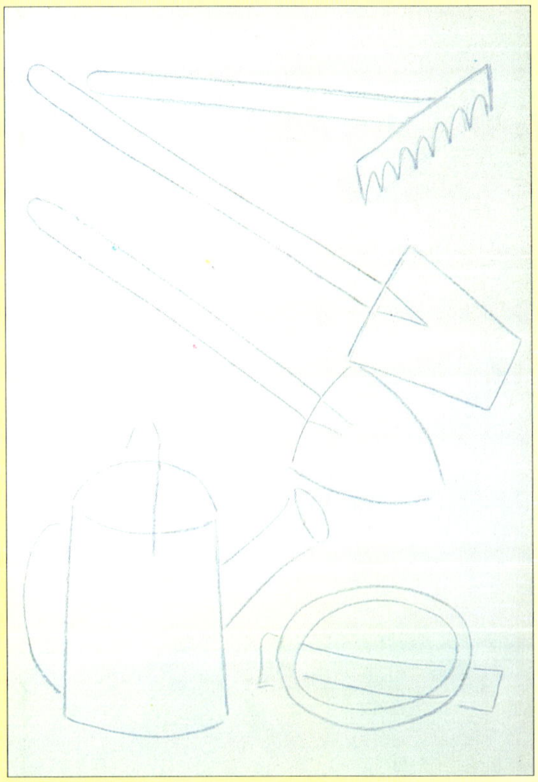

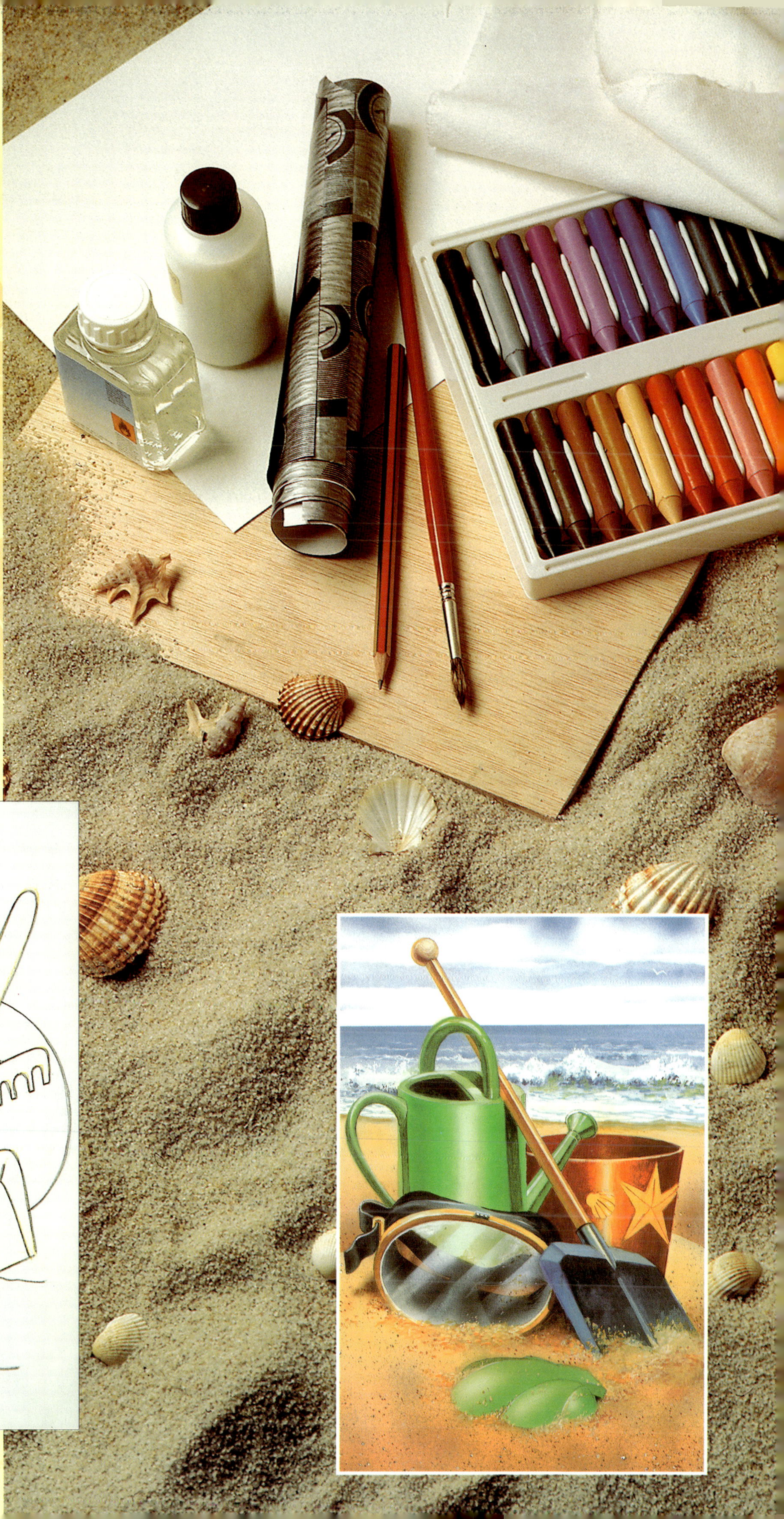

3 Add the details to your drawing.

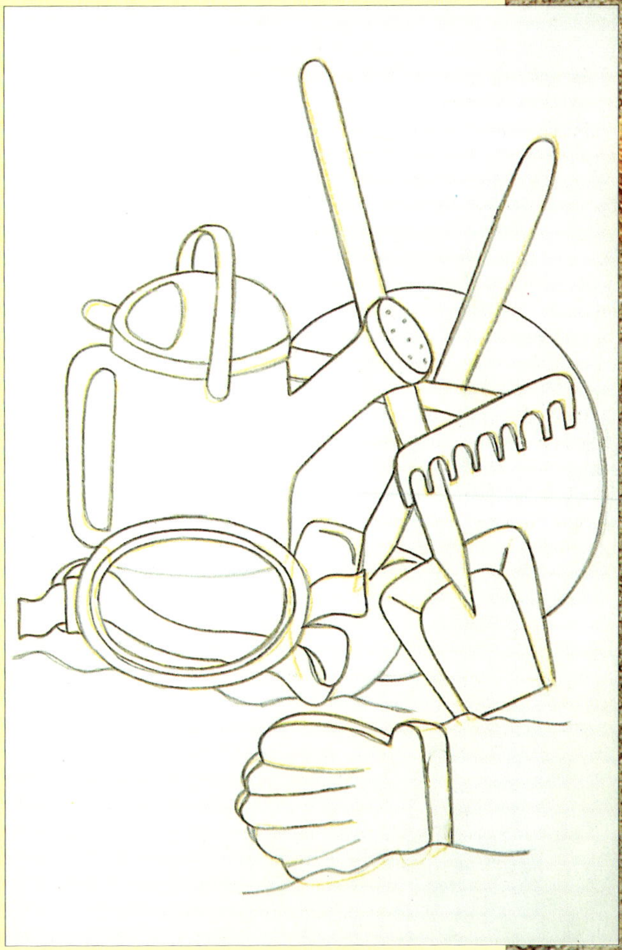

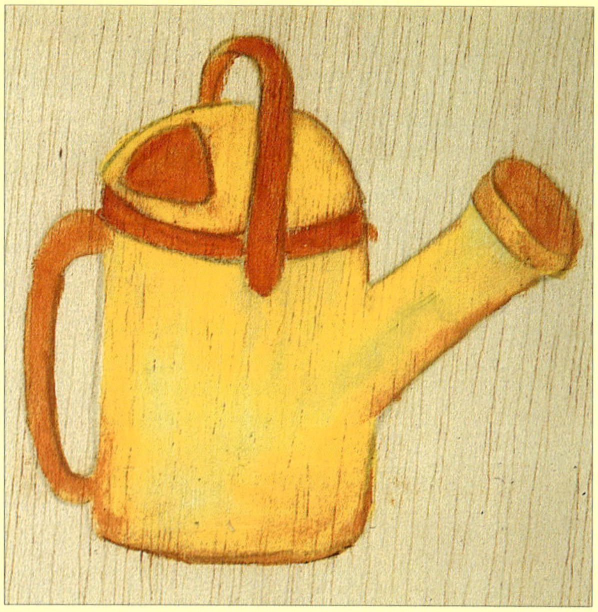

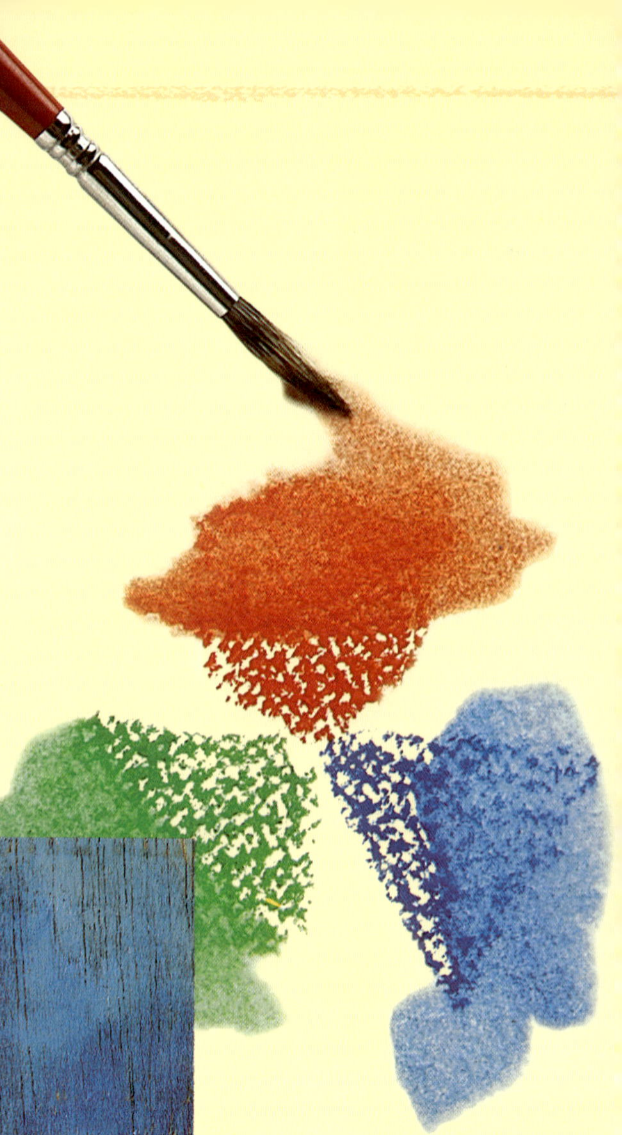

4 Transfer the drawing to a wooden board by using a sheet of black *carbon paper*. Color the image with wax crayons, working the dark tones over light ones to create *volume*.

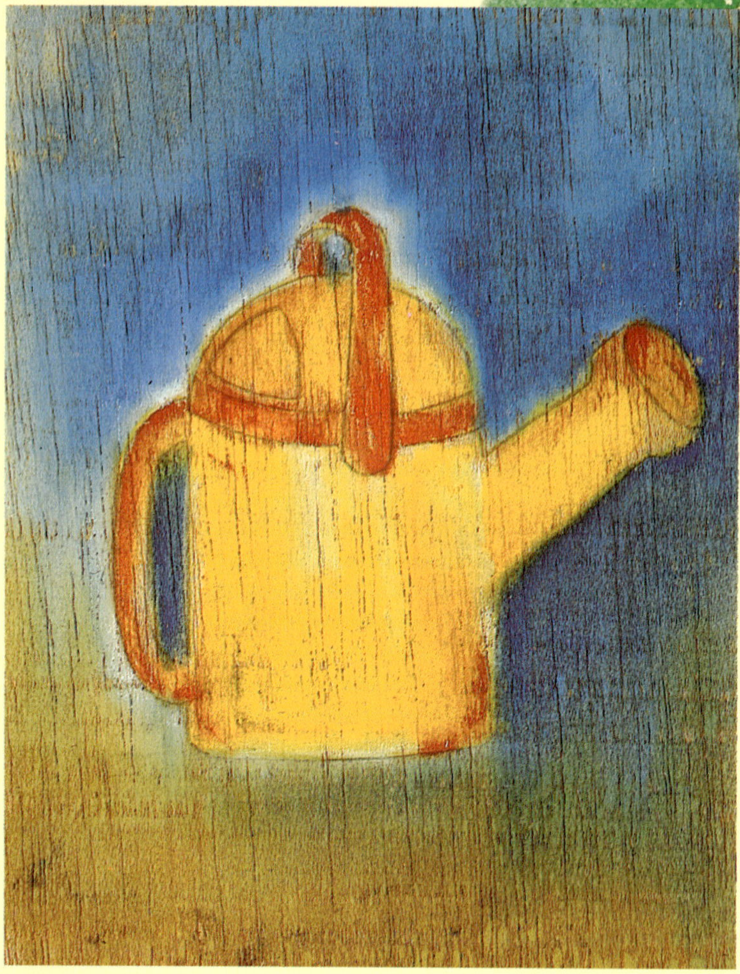

5 With a brush or the tip of a cloth moistened with a little turpentine, *dilute* the wax colors on the board to obtain a gradation of tones.

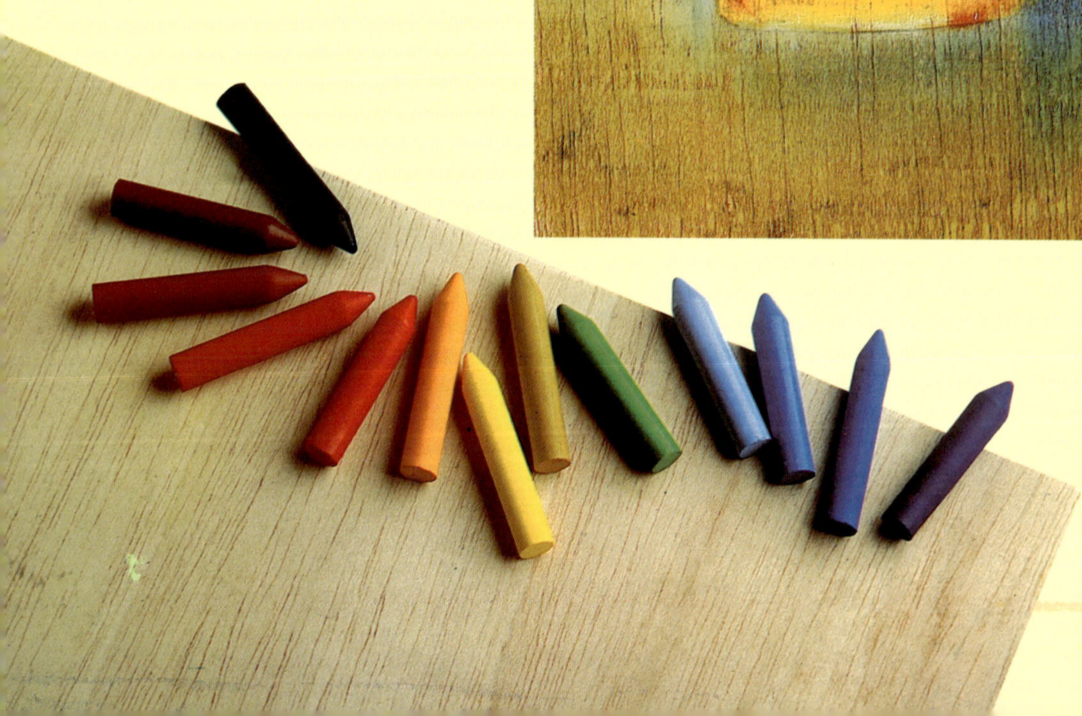

6 Dilute a little wax from a black crayon in turpentine and, with a brush, use it to emphasize the outline the *contours* of each element. You can apply an overall coat of all-purpose white glue thinned with water, which will serve as a fixative for your drawing.

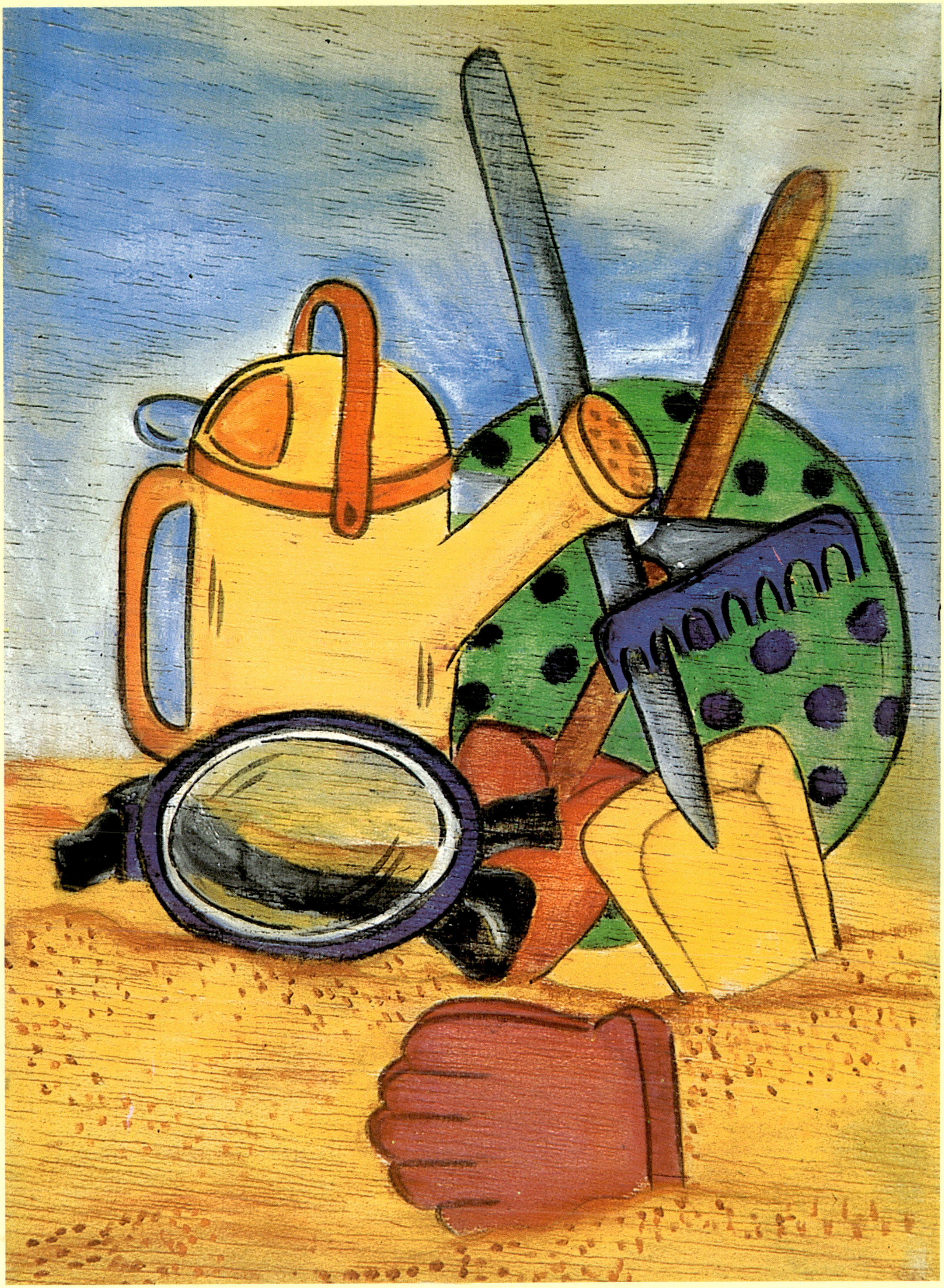

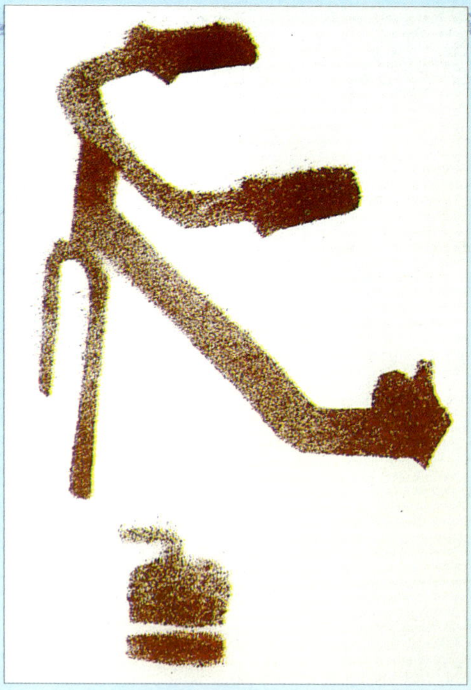

4 To give the object some volume, clean the brush with water and reload it with paint in a darker tone. Then repeat the spattering procedure over the shadow areas.

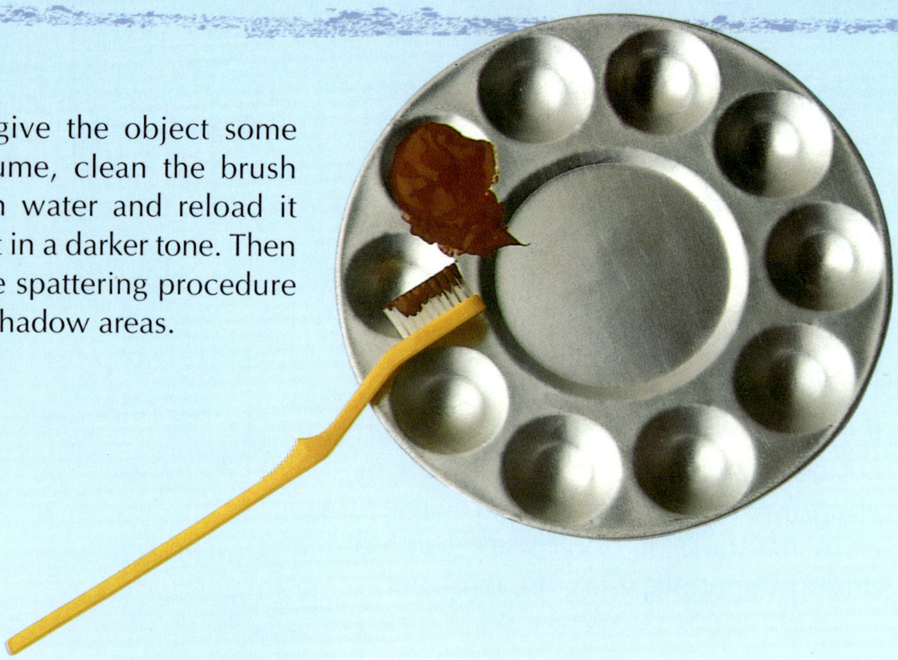

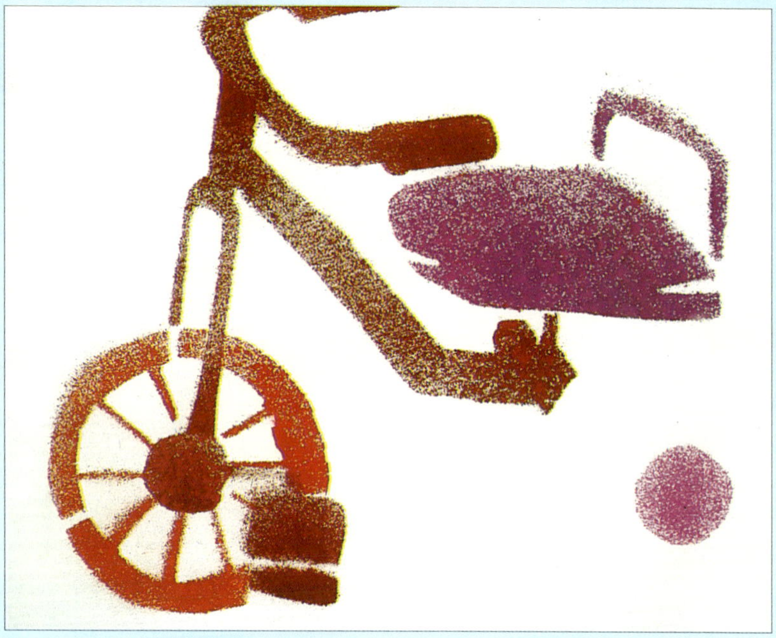

5 After the paint dries, place the stencil on the paper for the next element of the object. Line up the edges of the stencil with those of the image on the paper, load the brush with the new color, and again spatter the paint on the paper.

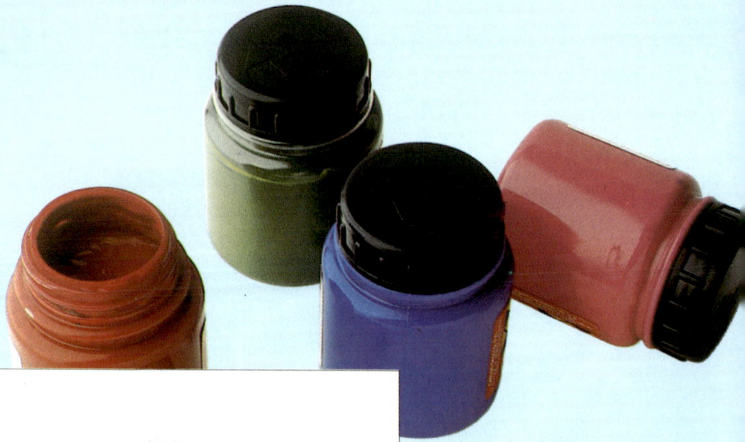

6 To make the tricycle seat stand out, paint some polka-dots on it.

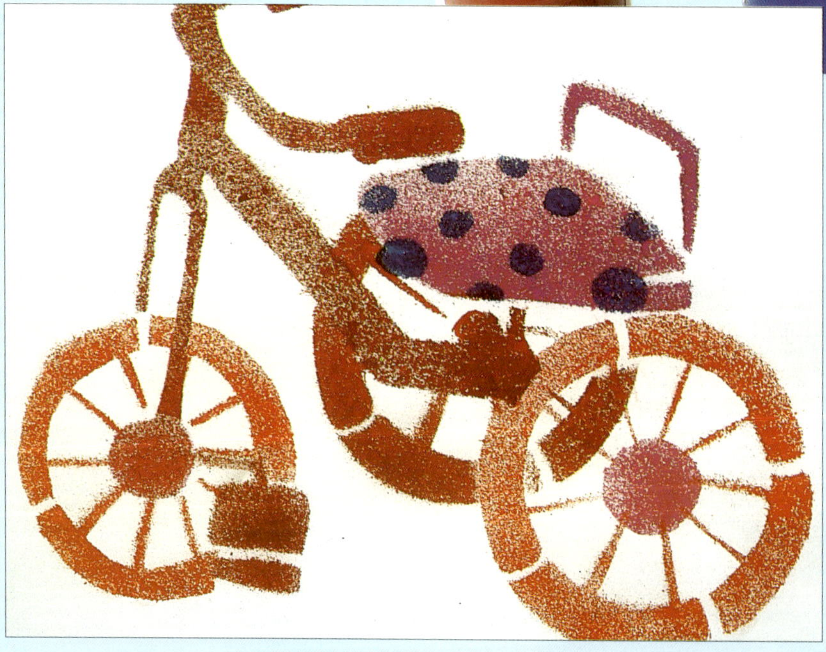

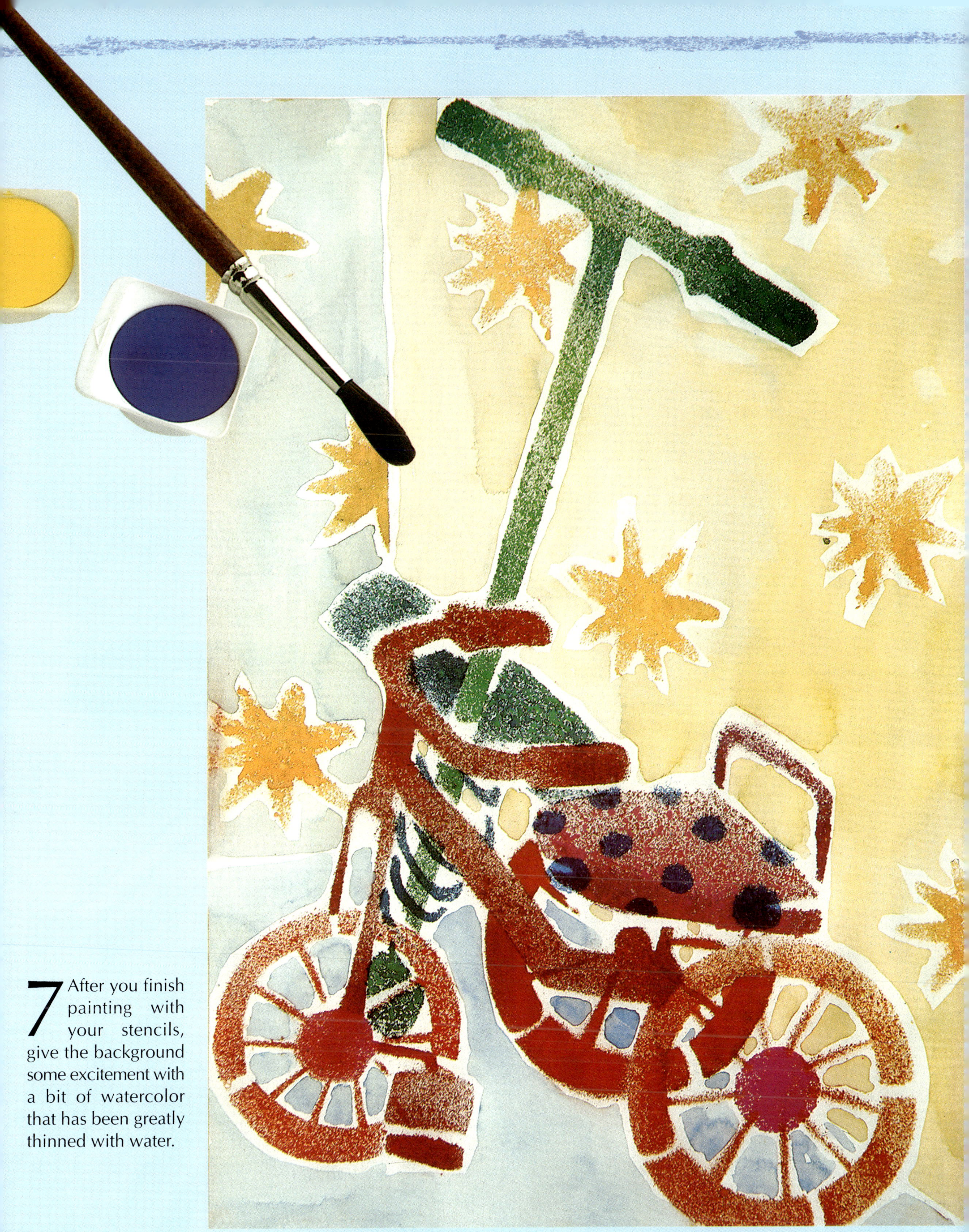

7 After you finish painting with your stencils, give the background some excitement with a bit of watercolor that has been greatly thinned with water.

A Dining Room Collage

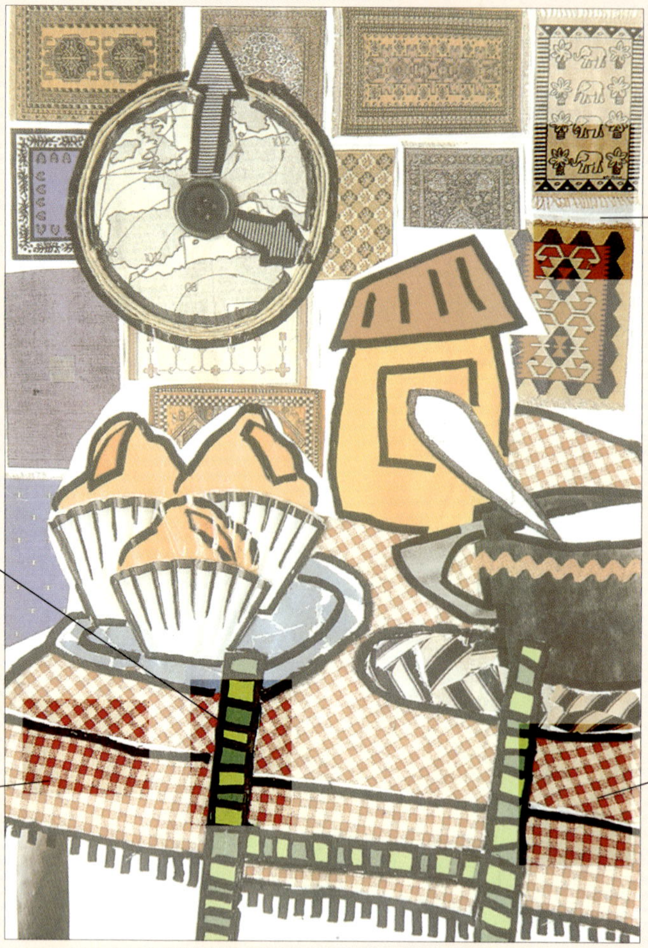

Have you painted a picture on paper and been disappointed by the results? Don't throw it away! You may be able to use parts of it to create a *collage*.

When applying a coat of glue to a piece of paper or cloth, spread the glue well from the center to the outer edges to avoid using too much.

To clearly separate the different objects, use materials with highly contrasted designs.

The illusion of depth can be created by placing the same material in a different position.

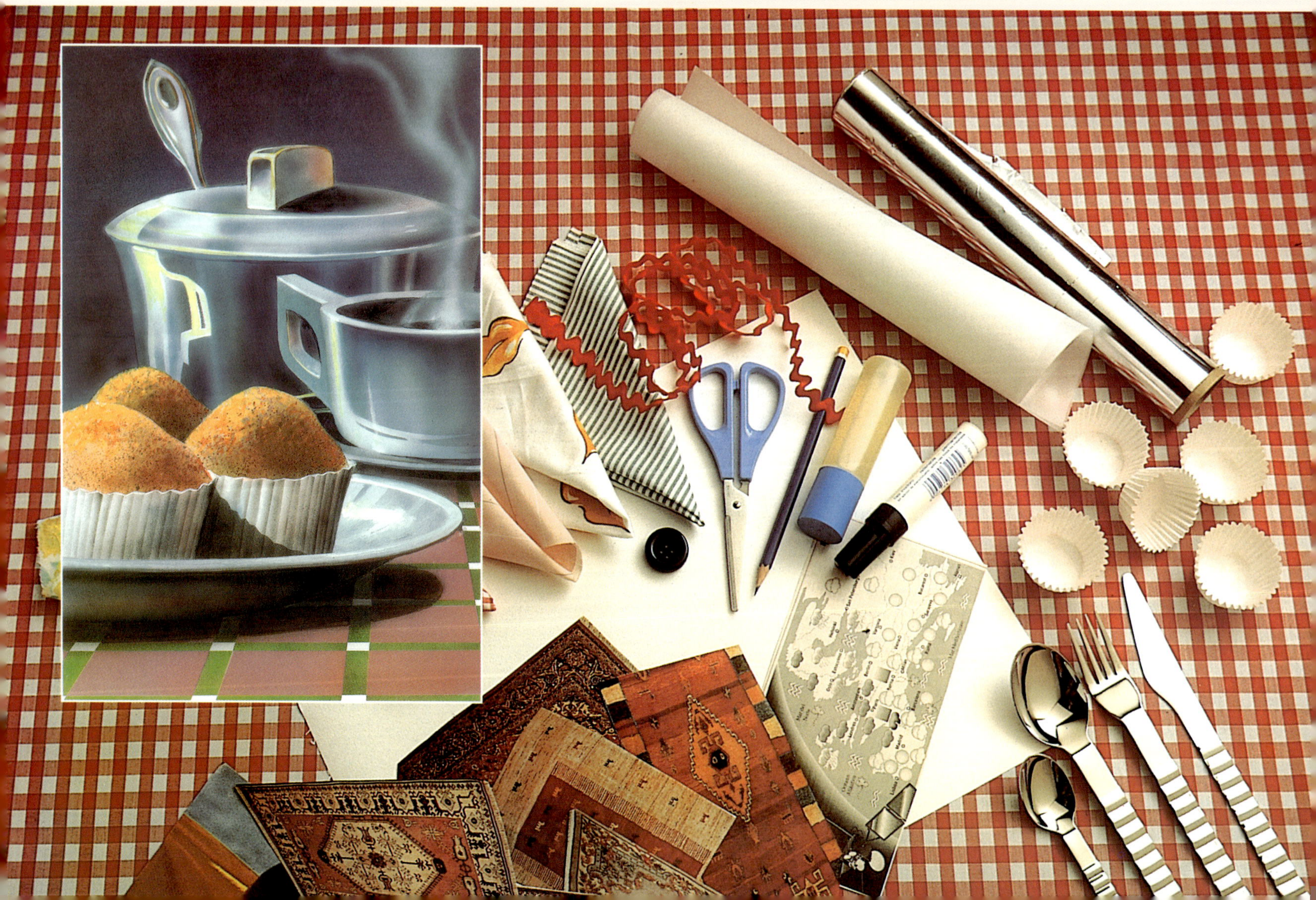

1 Draw a form sketch of your objects.

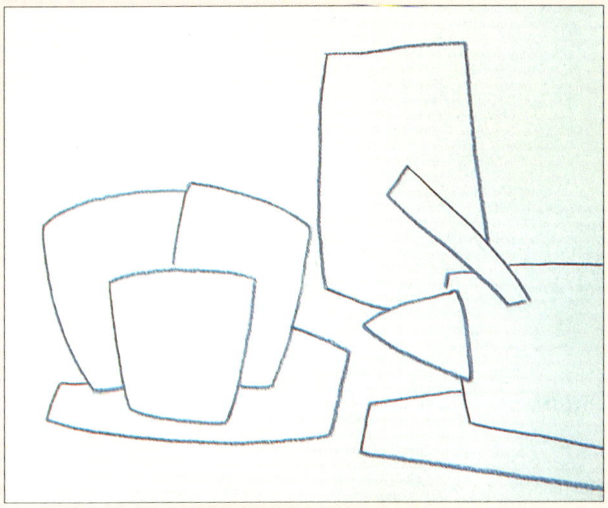

2 Sketch and format your composition.

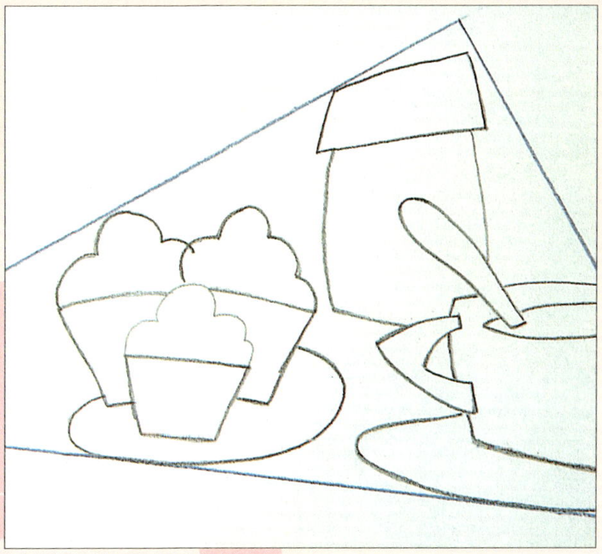

Materials and Techniques

You can ensure that the pieces of material you cut will perfectly match your drawing. First draw the outline of each element on tracing paper. Then, use this paper outline as a pattern for cutting the material.

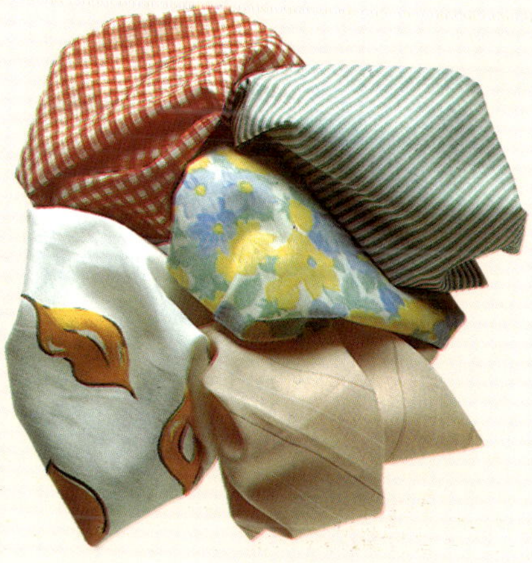

3 Finish your drawing. Search for materials with interesting patterns—such as torn pieces of fabric, waste cardboard, newspapers, magazines, yarn, and so on.

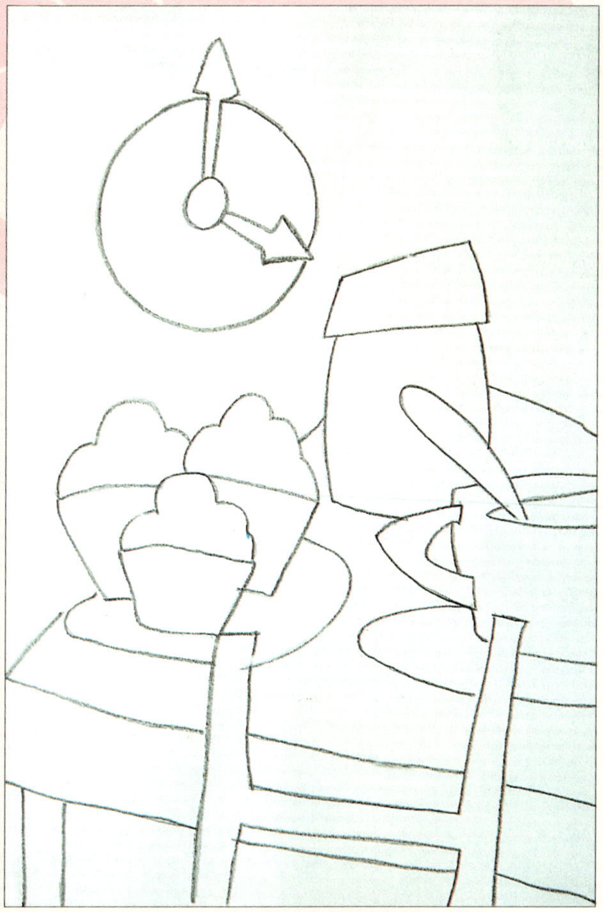

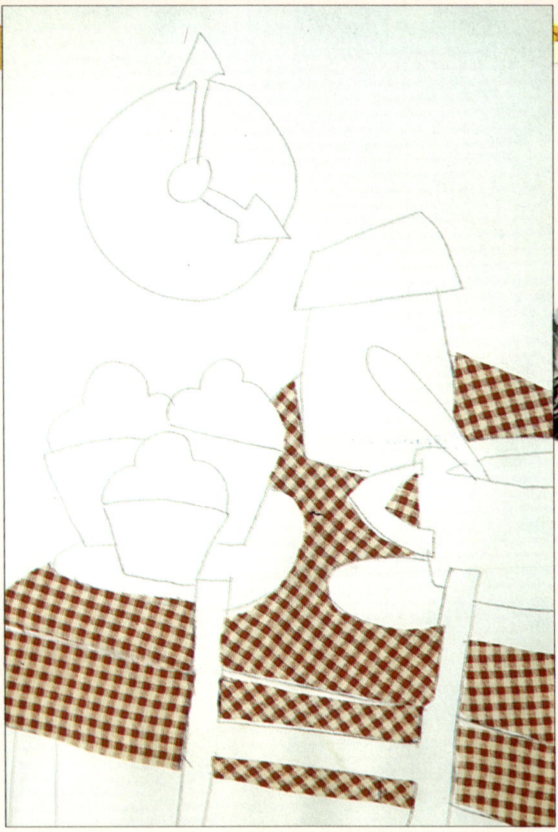

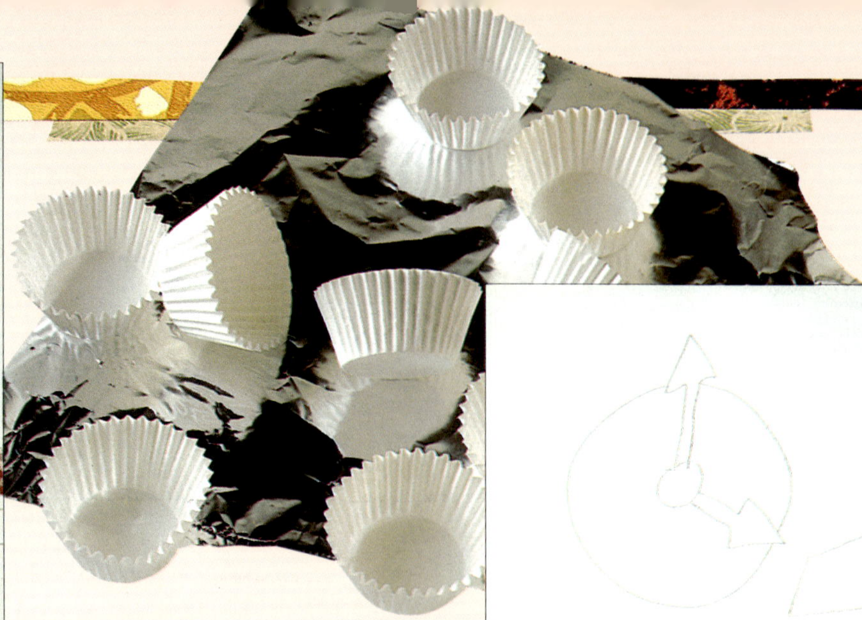

5 Use primary colors in the areas that you don't want to cover with material.

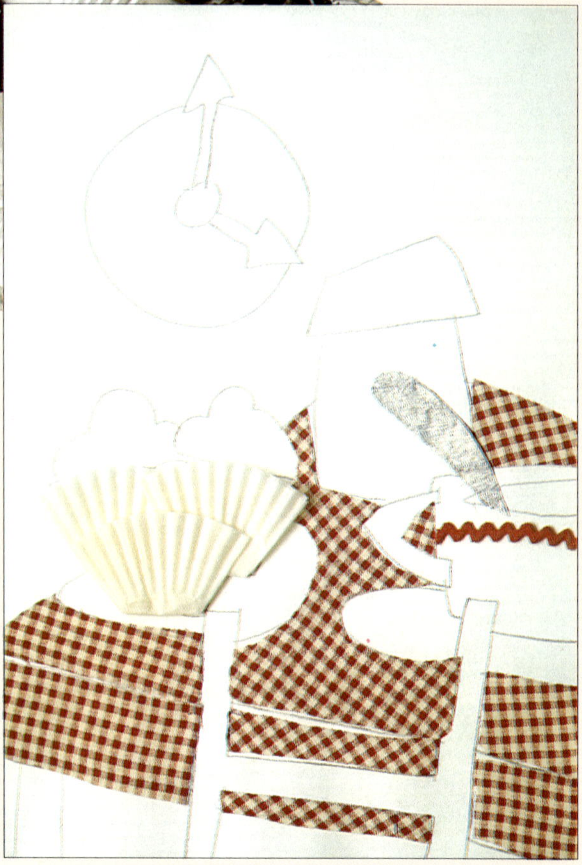

4 Choose the materials that will better suit your composition. Here, we have selected a scrap of checkered fabric for our tablecloth. After trimming the fabric, attach it to the picture surface with all-purpose white glue.

6 Finish gluing the rest of the materials to your collage. Play around with the textures to find startling and funny effects. For example, scraps of printed fabrics could be used on the porcelain plates.

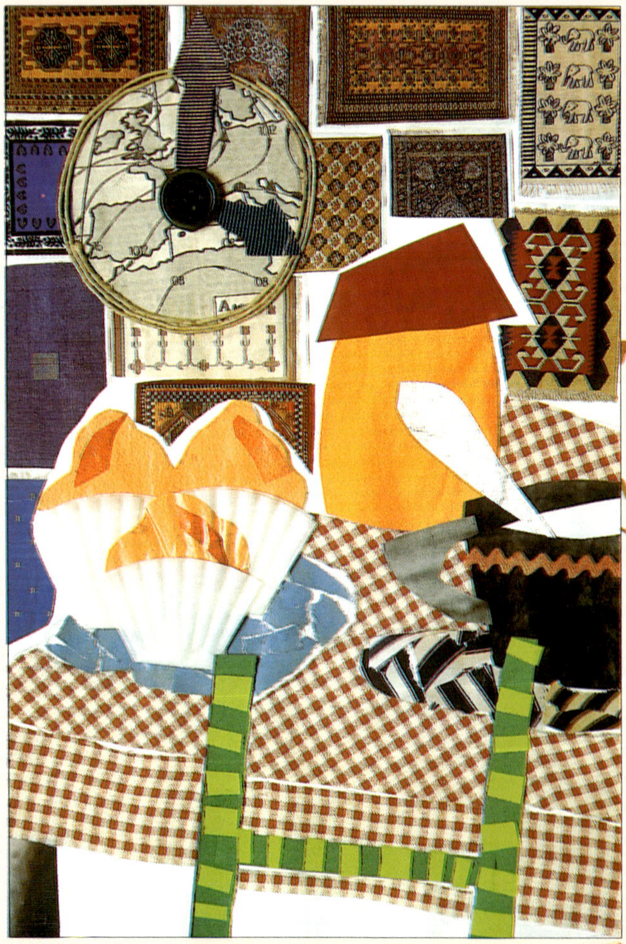

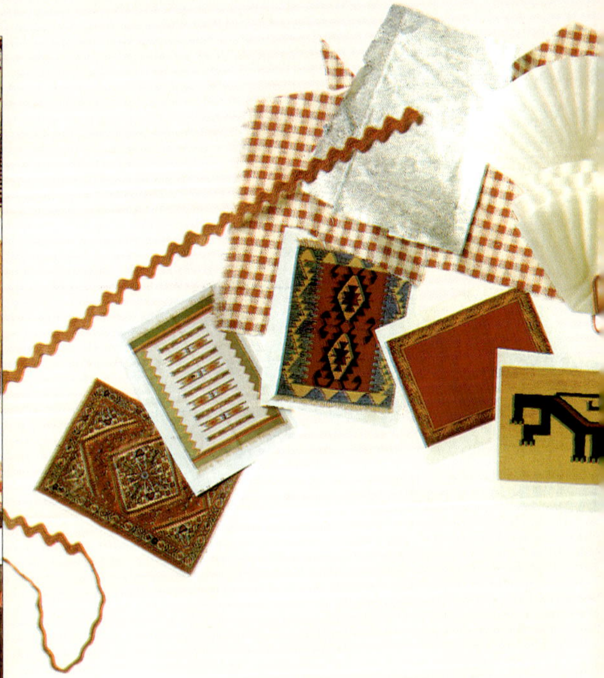

7 Finally, with a thick marker, outline some elements and add a few finishing touches.

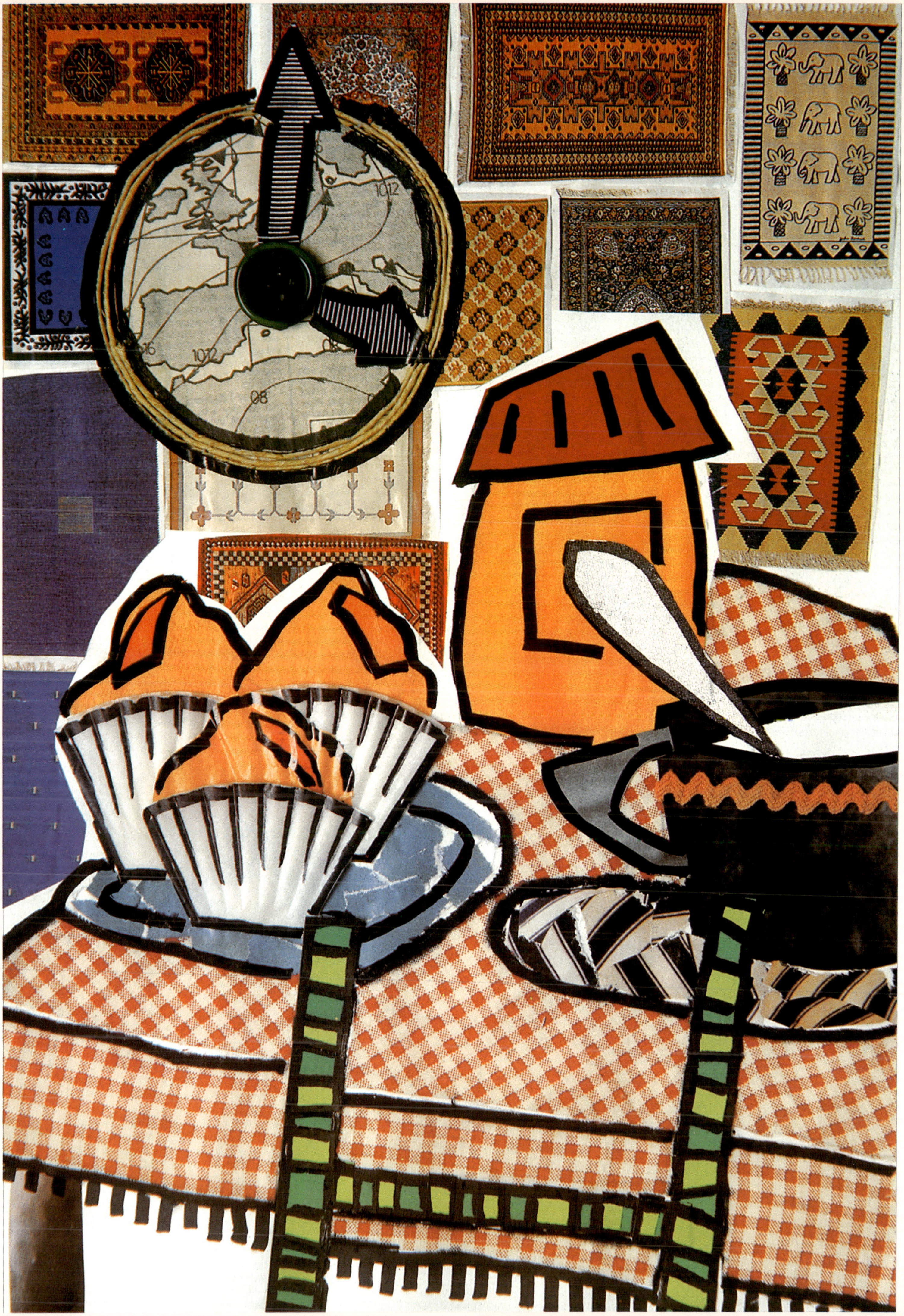

A Symphony in Gold and Silver Paper

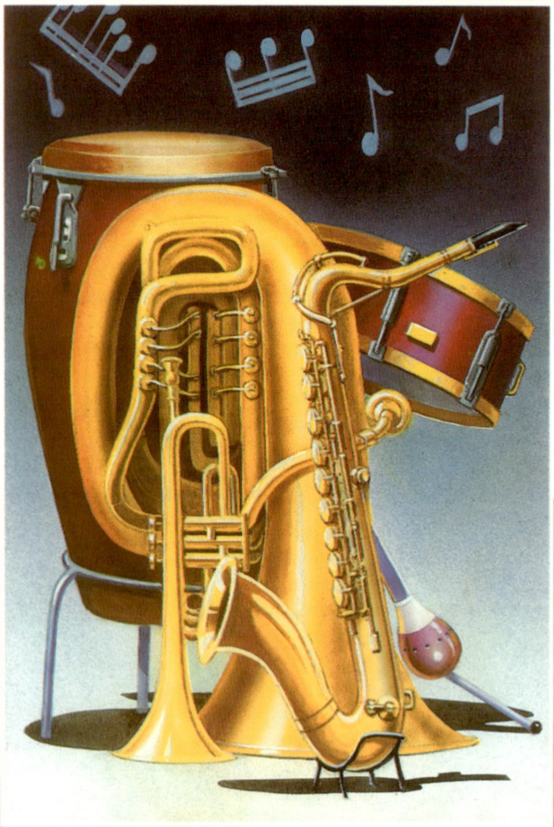

Metallic objects are ideal subjects for this technique. The gold and silver paper capture the effect of light reflecting from the metal.

This drawing will be done with a black background, but the technique works with any dark color.

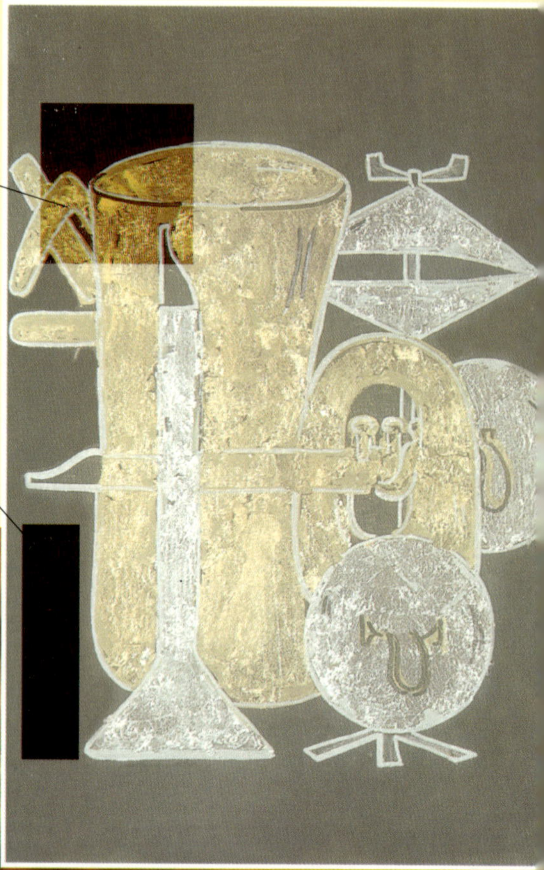

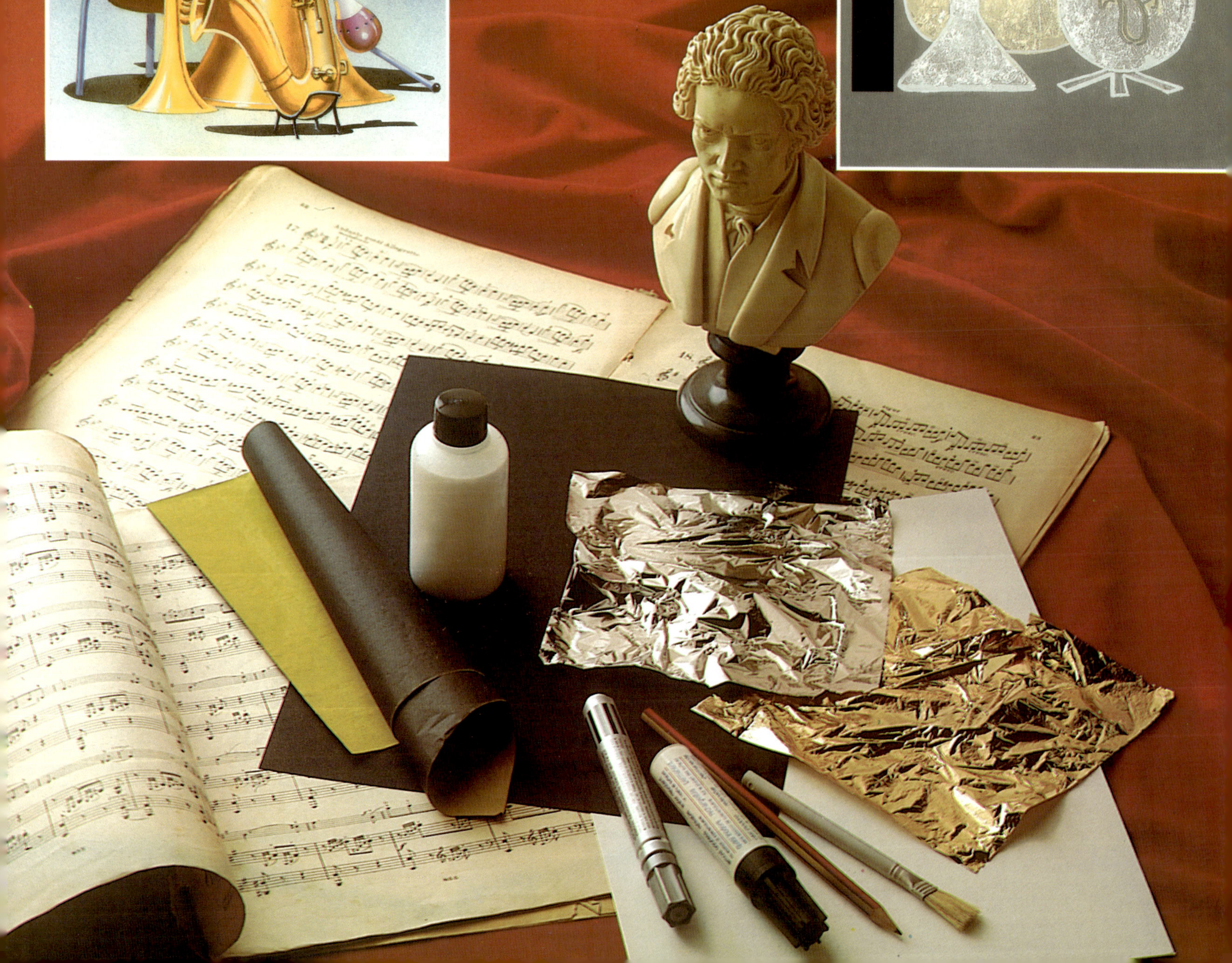

1 After preparing the form sketch, arrange the objects to create your composition.

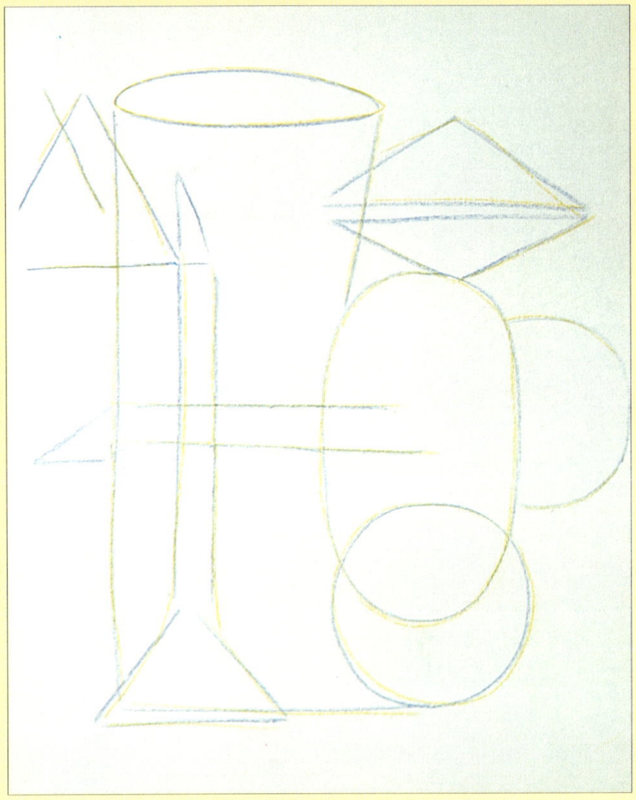

Materials and Techniques

Silver and gold paper sheets are available from any art supply store. But kitchen-type aluminum foil and gold gift wrapping can also be used.

2 Here, we have placed the objects within a square format and centered the image on the sheet of paper.

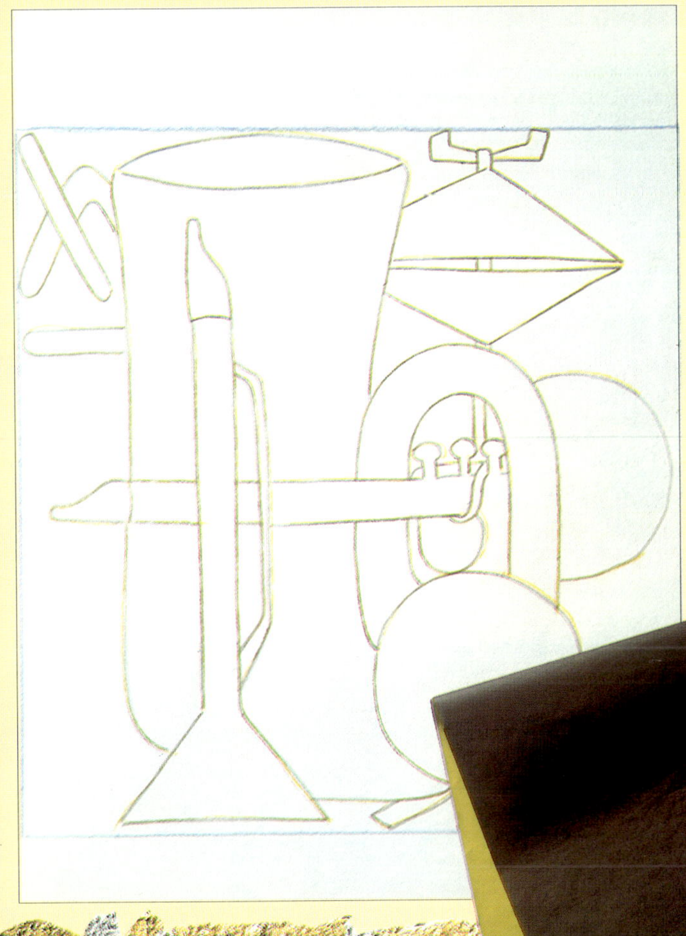

3 Using light-colored carbon paper, transfer your drawing to a black background. If you can't get light-colored carbon paper, cover the back of your drawing with yellow crayon. Then, go over the lines of the drawing with a pencil to transfer them to the black surface.

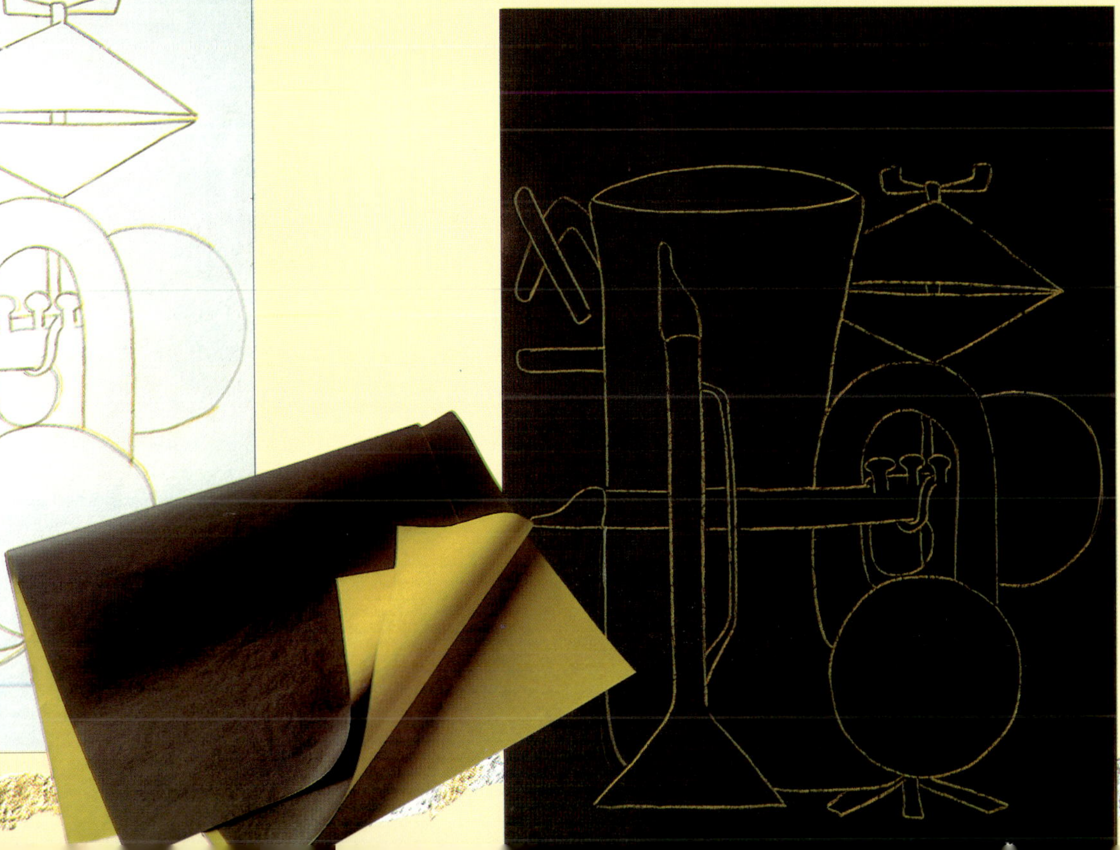

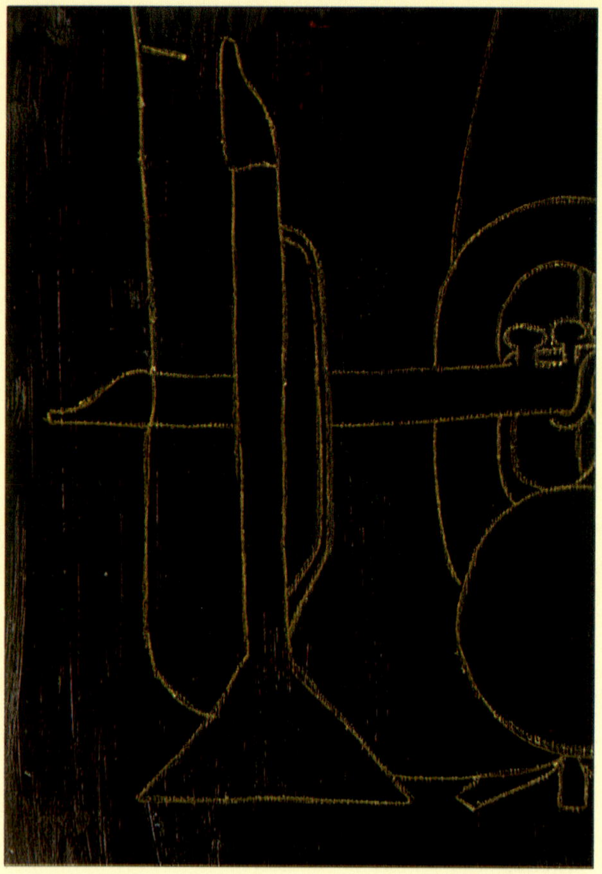

4 Coat the whole surface with water-thinned white glue and allow it to dry.

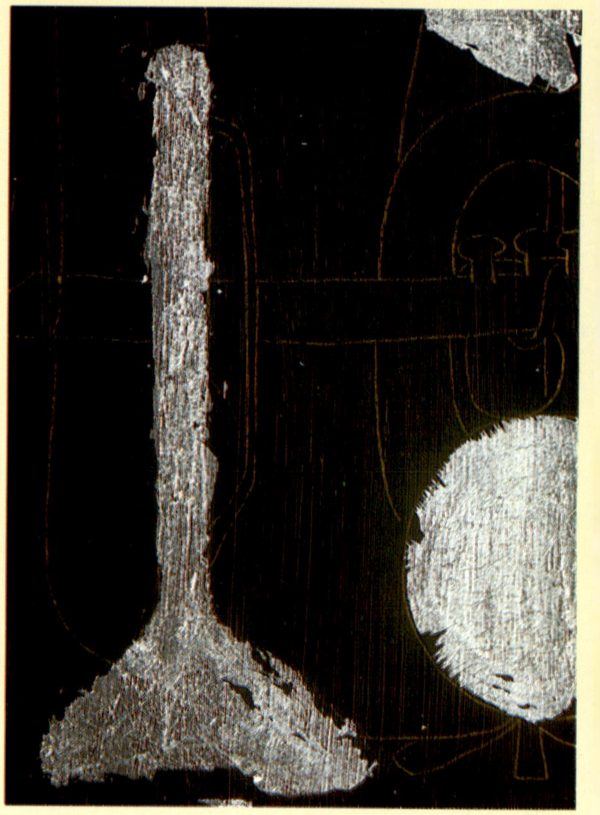

5 Next, apply glue again, but only on the areas you want to cover with silver paper. When the glue is partially dry, paste the paper to the surface by gently pressing on it until it is secured.

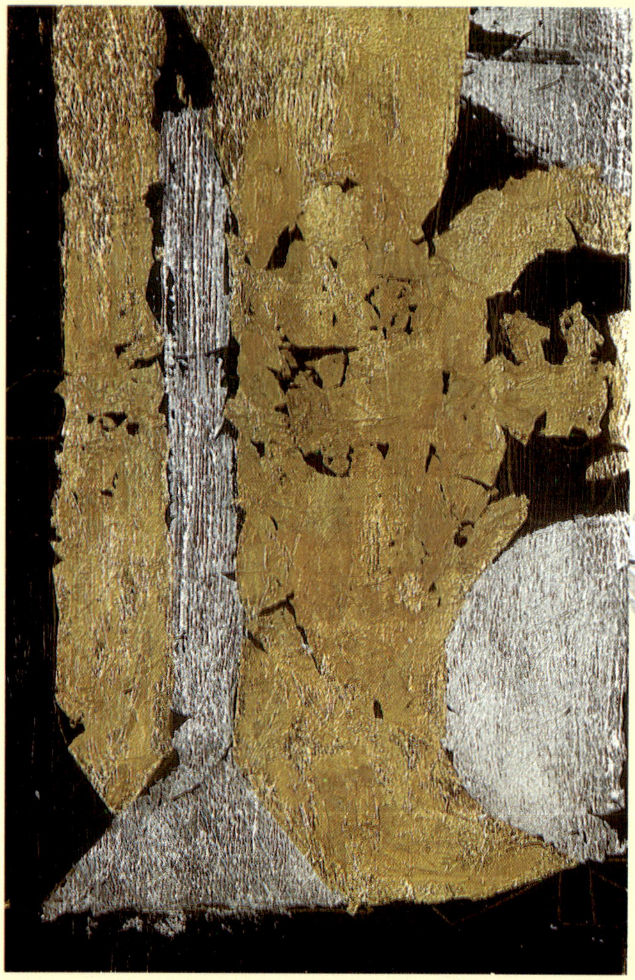

6 After gluing the silver sheets, repeat the procedure with the gold paper.

7 Finish your picture by outlining the objects with a silver marker and creating some reflections with a black marker.

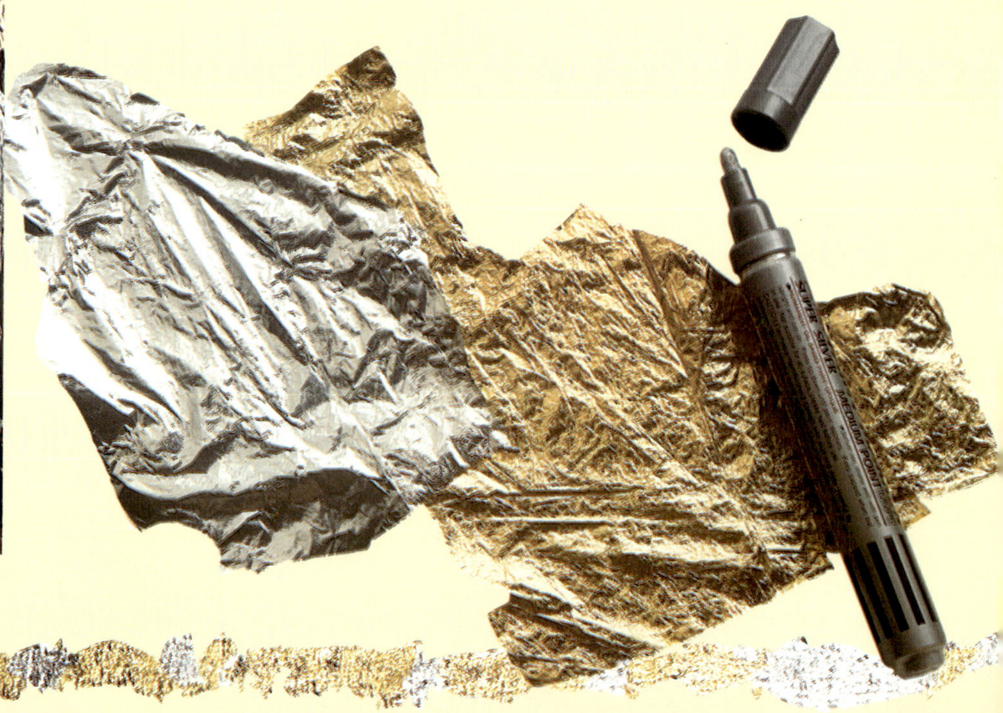

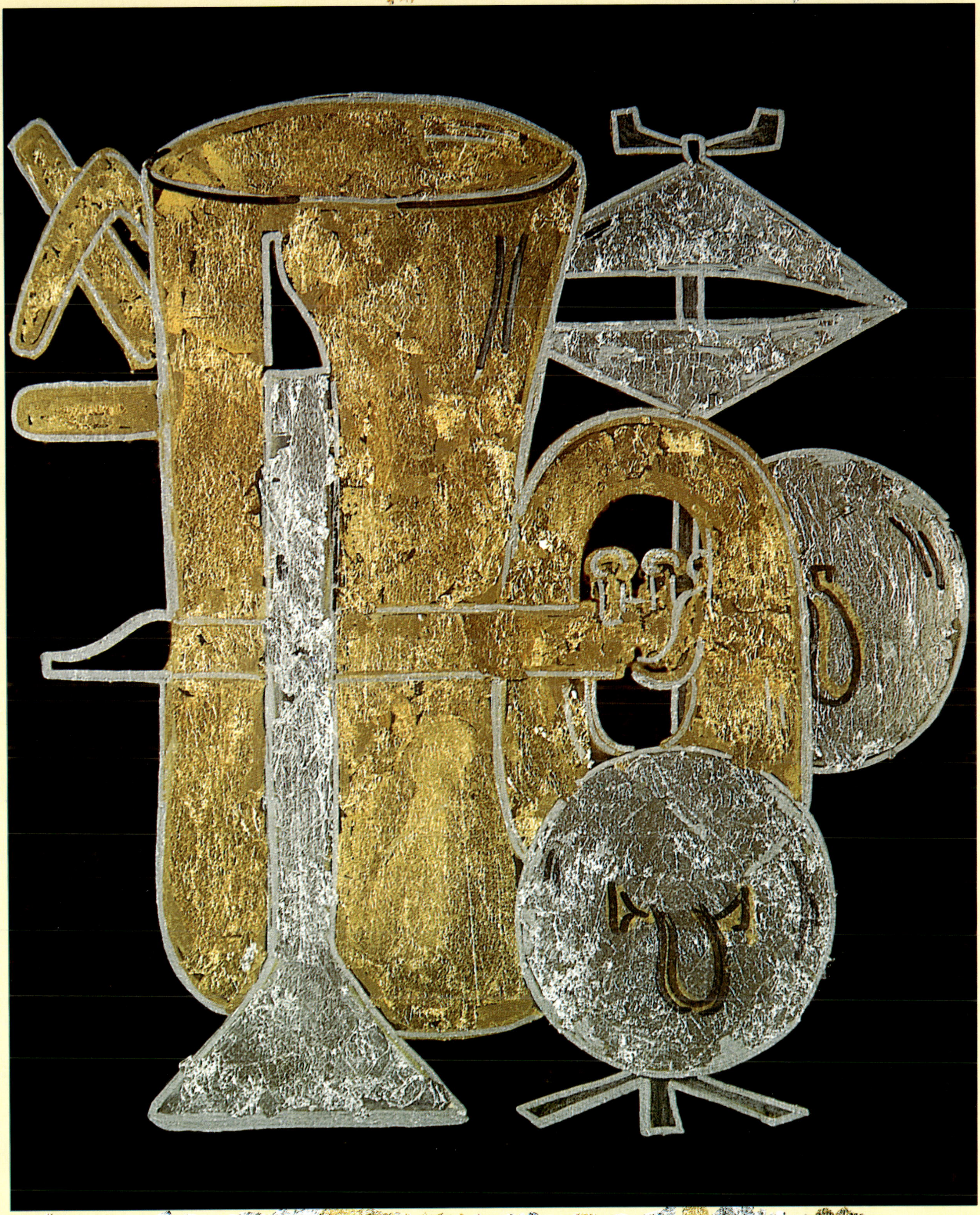

In-Line Skates with Texture

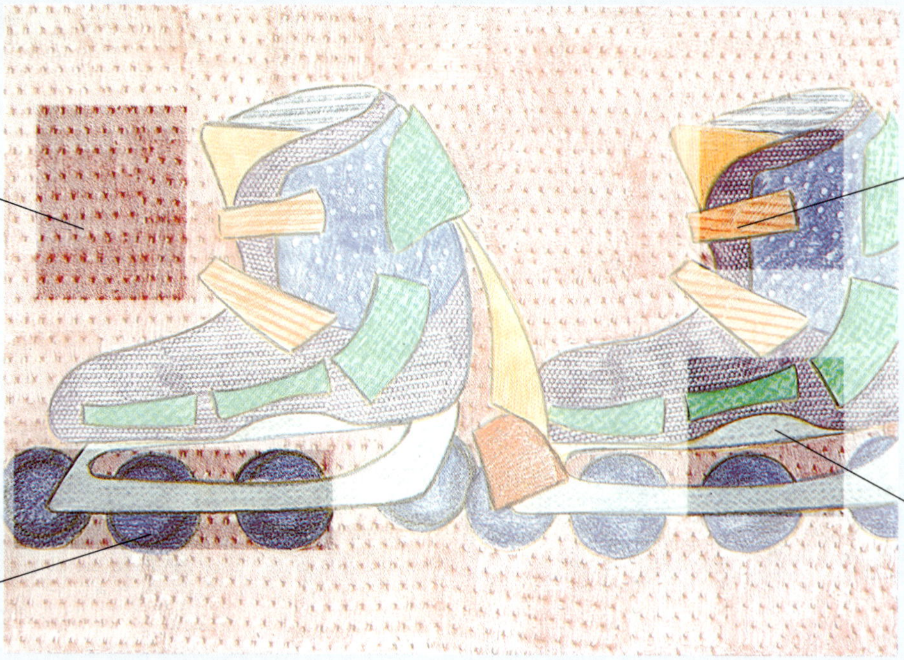

The background is painted in a single color and pattern. This makes the drawing stand out.

Different textures add interest and richness to a drawing.

Groups of related elements are done in the same color and texture to tie them together.

Drawing very small elements should be avoided because it would be difficult to paint them in a textured pattern.

Useful Tips

The appeal and richness of a drawing will depend on the variety of textural patterns it contains. Search for objects with different textures and try their effects on your drawing.

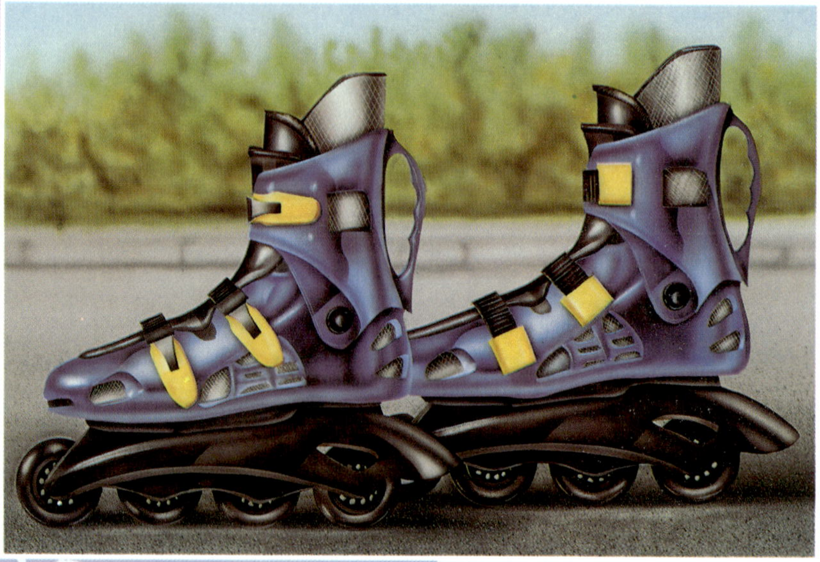

1 As always, begin with a form sketch of the objects in the drawing.

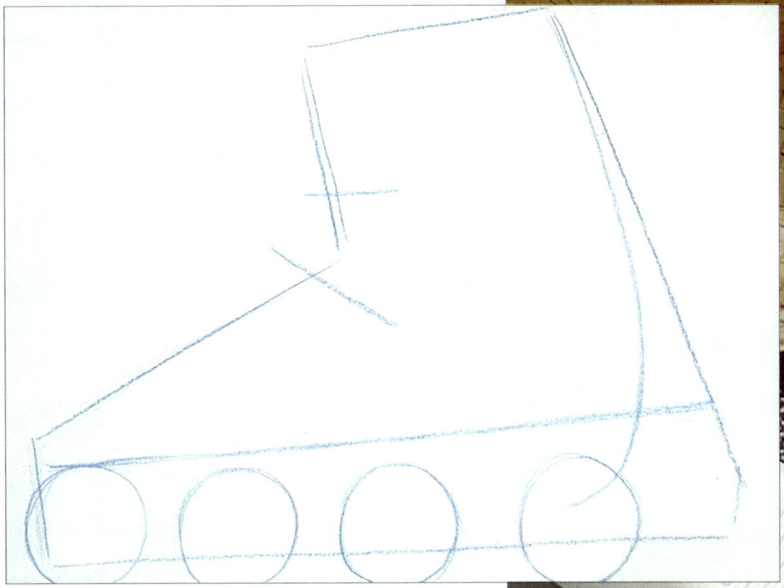

2 Add the lines that fill in the details.

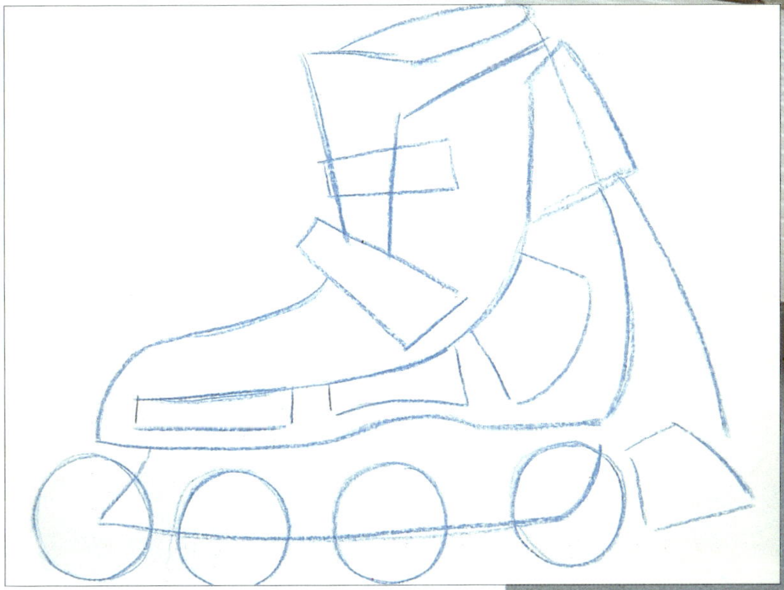

3 Arrange your composition on the final sheet of paper and remember to outline each area to mark the limits of the textural patterns.

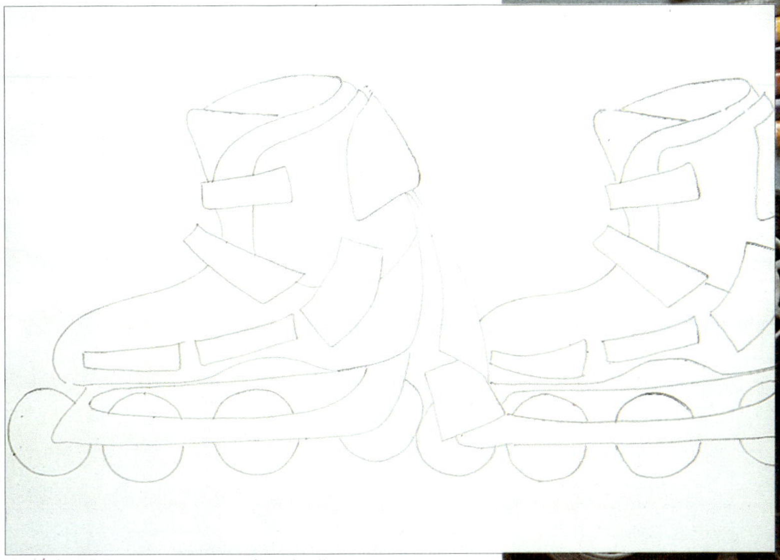

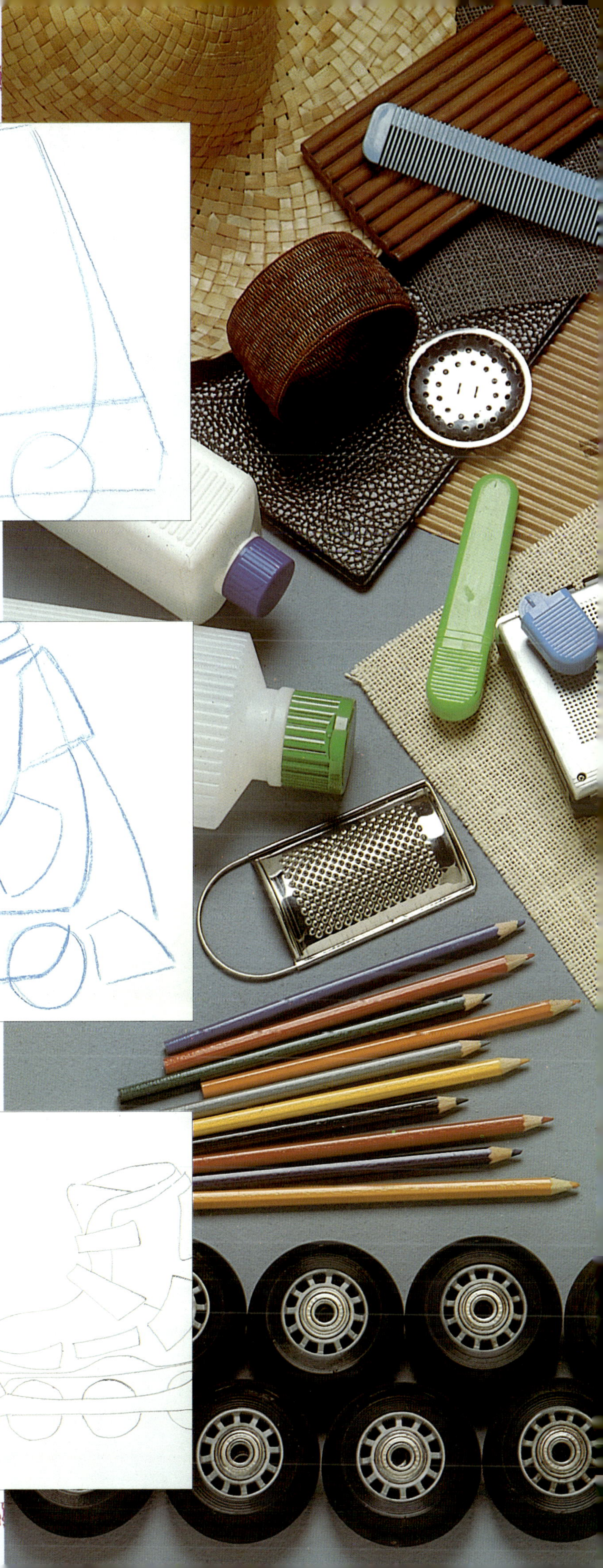

4 On a separate sheet of paper (of the same type you are using for your drawing) try the textural patterns that result from working colored pencils over materials of different textures—such as a straw hat, corrugated cardboard, a grater, and so on. The following page illustrates examples of the different textures that can be obtained.

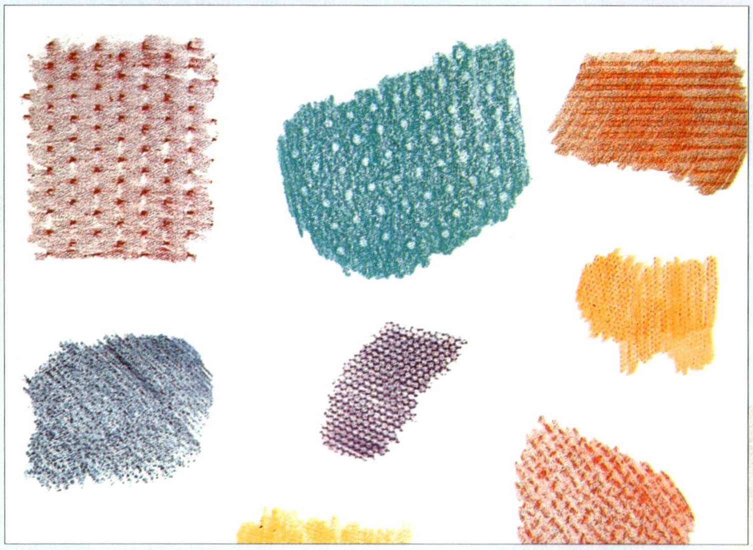

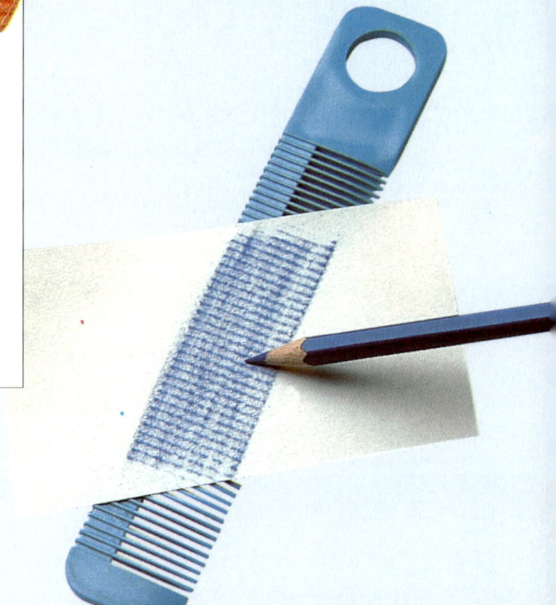

5 After selecting the area and the color for each pattern, place the paper over the textured object and fill in the area with the chosen color. Try to use the same texture for all the similar elements in your drawing.

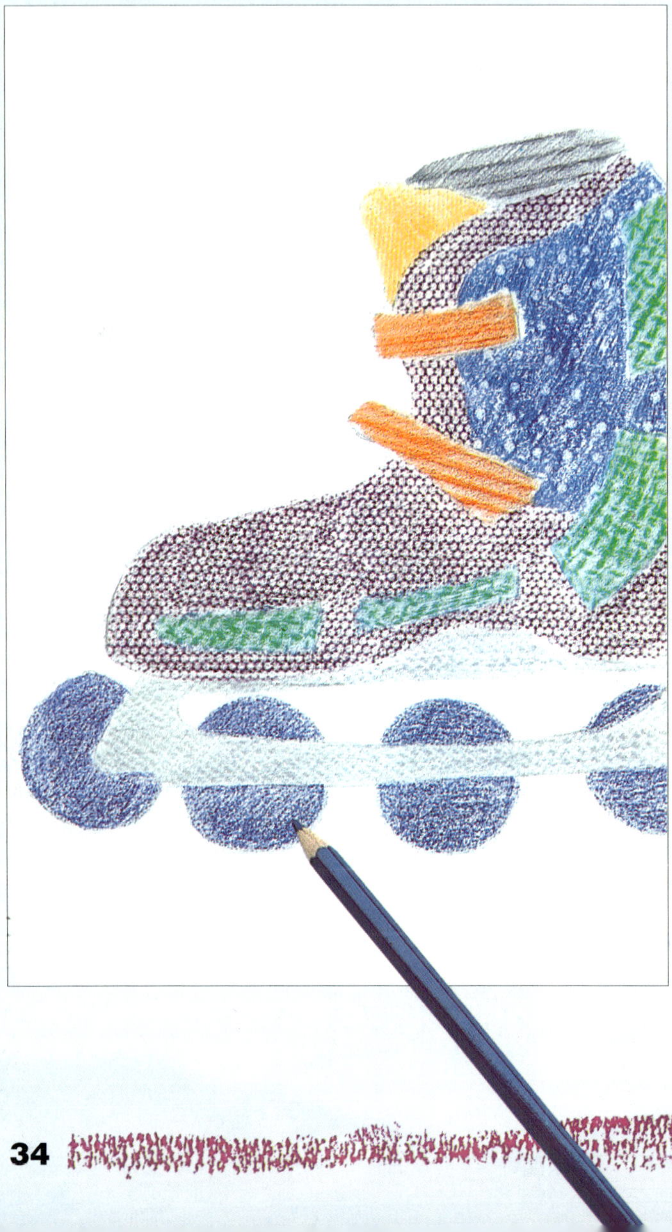

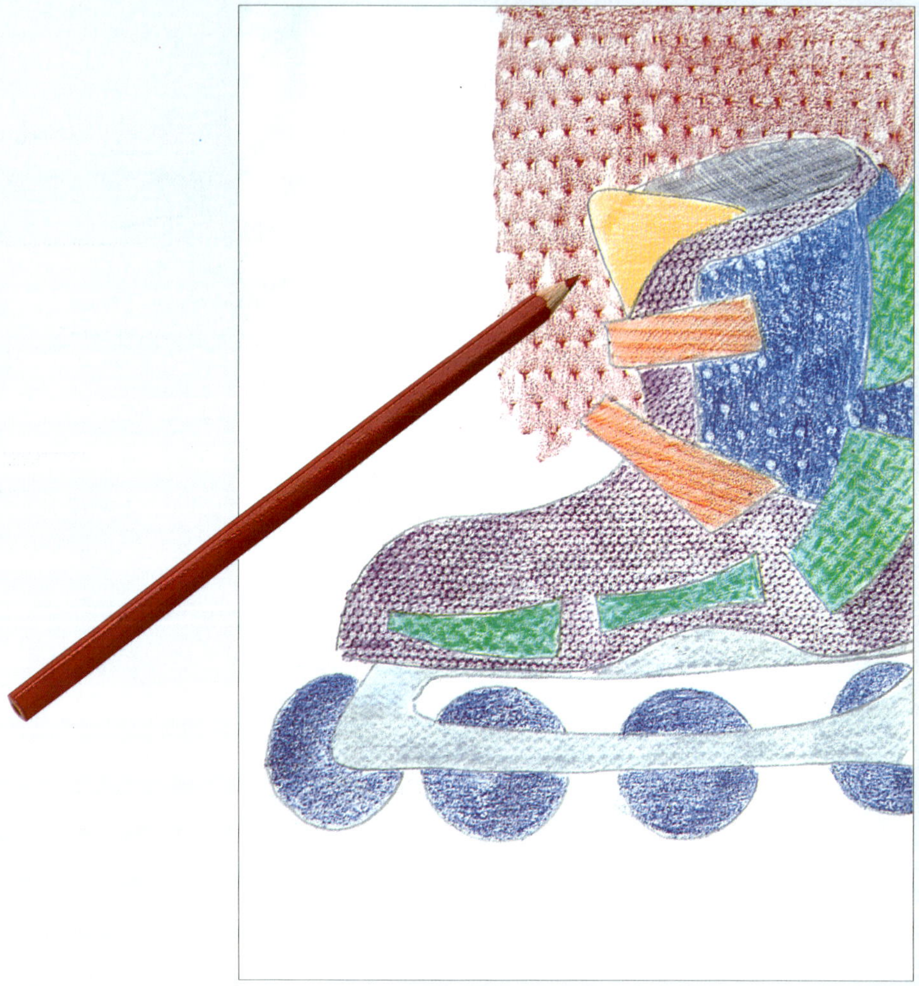

6 Your drawing now has plenty of color and texture, so do the background in a single color.

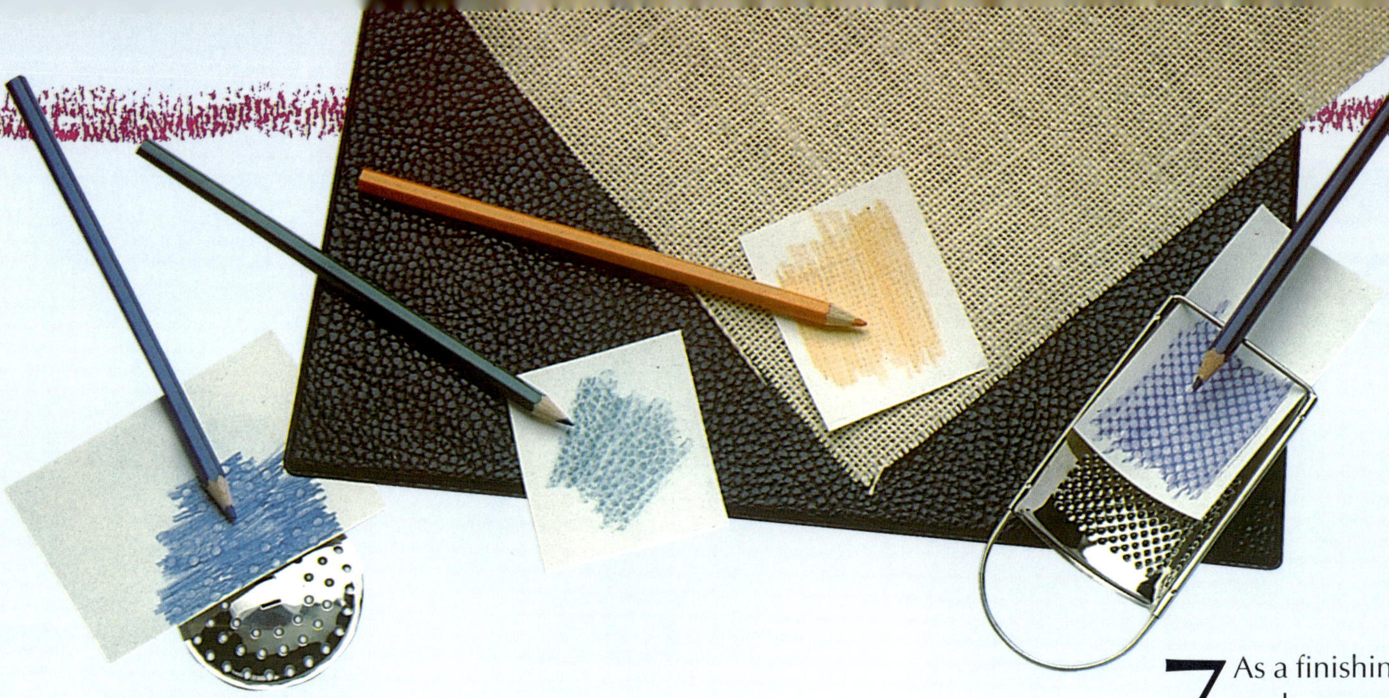

7 As a finishing touch, outline each area with a different color.

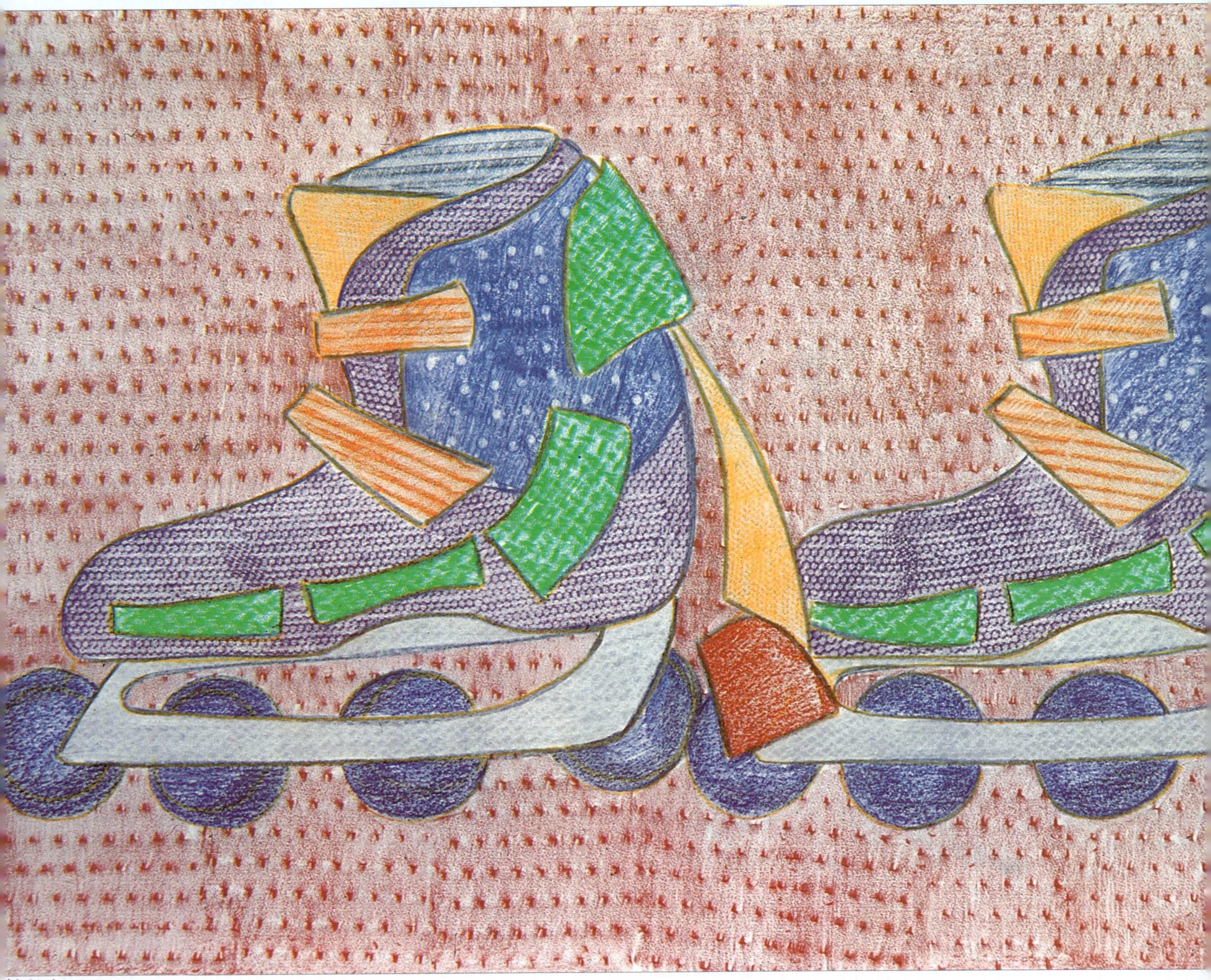

Ice Cream and Soda Done with Wax Crayons and Watercolors

Wax crayon is used to create the design patterns.

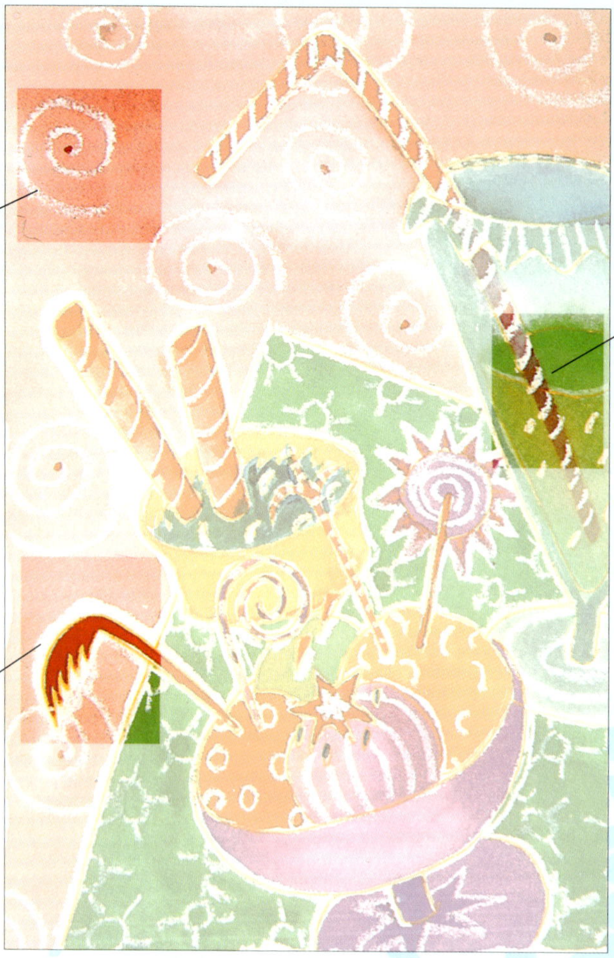

With watercolors, a gradation is obtained by applying a light tone followed by a dark one while the surface is still wet.

Outlining the objects with a wax crayon will keep the water-colors from mixing.

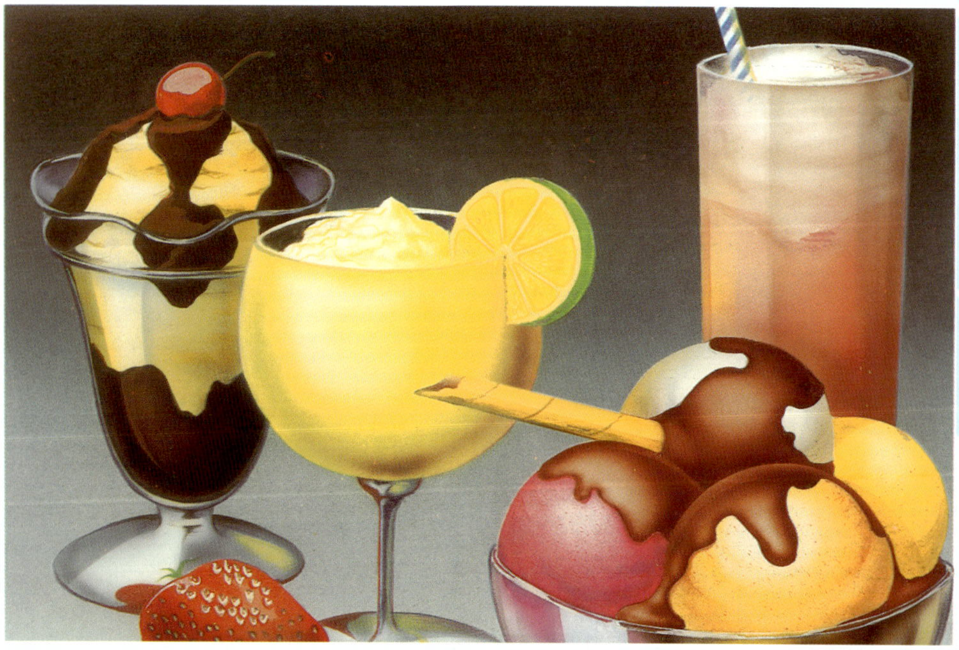

Materials and Techniques

With the blade of a round-tipped knife, the wax crayon must be repeatedly sharpened. This will keep the lines in the drawing clean and crisp.

1 Form-sketch and draw the objects.

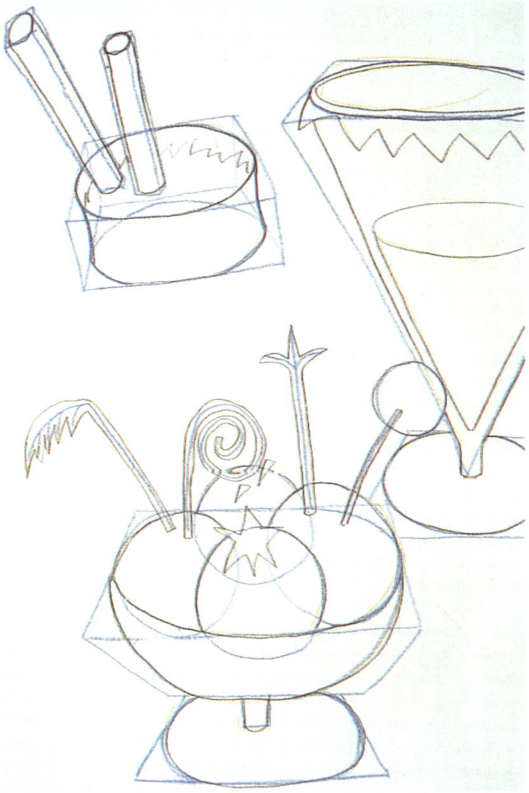

2 Arrange your composition. Here, parts of some objects have been cut off to create a sense of continuity. Use yellow crayon to trace the lines and don't apply too much pressure; you don't want the lines to show too much.

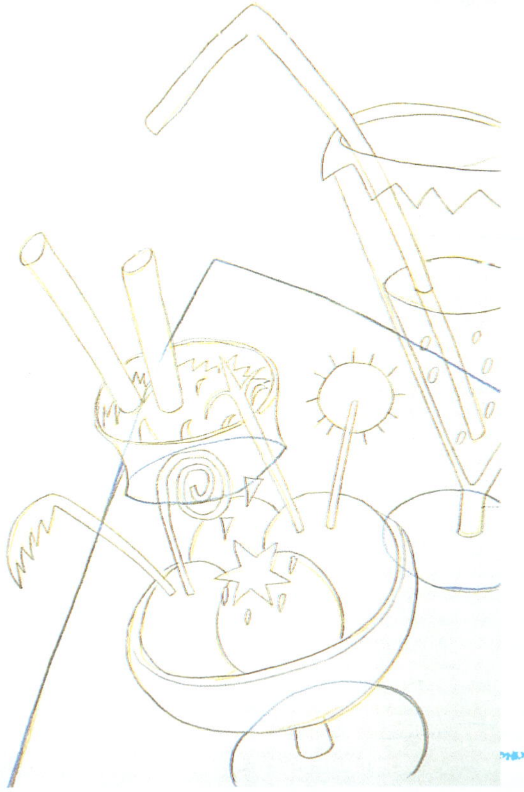

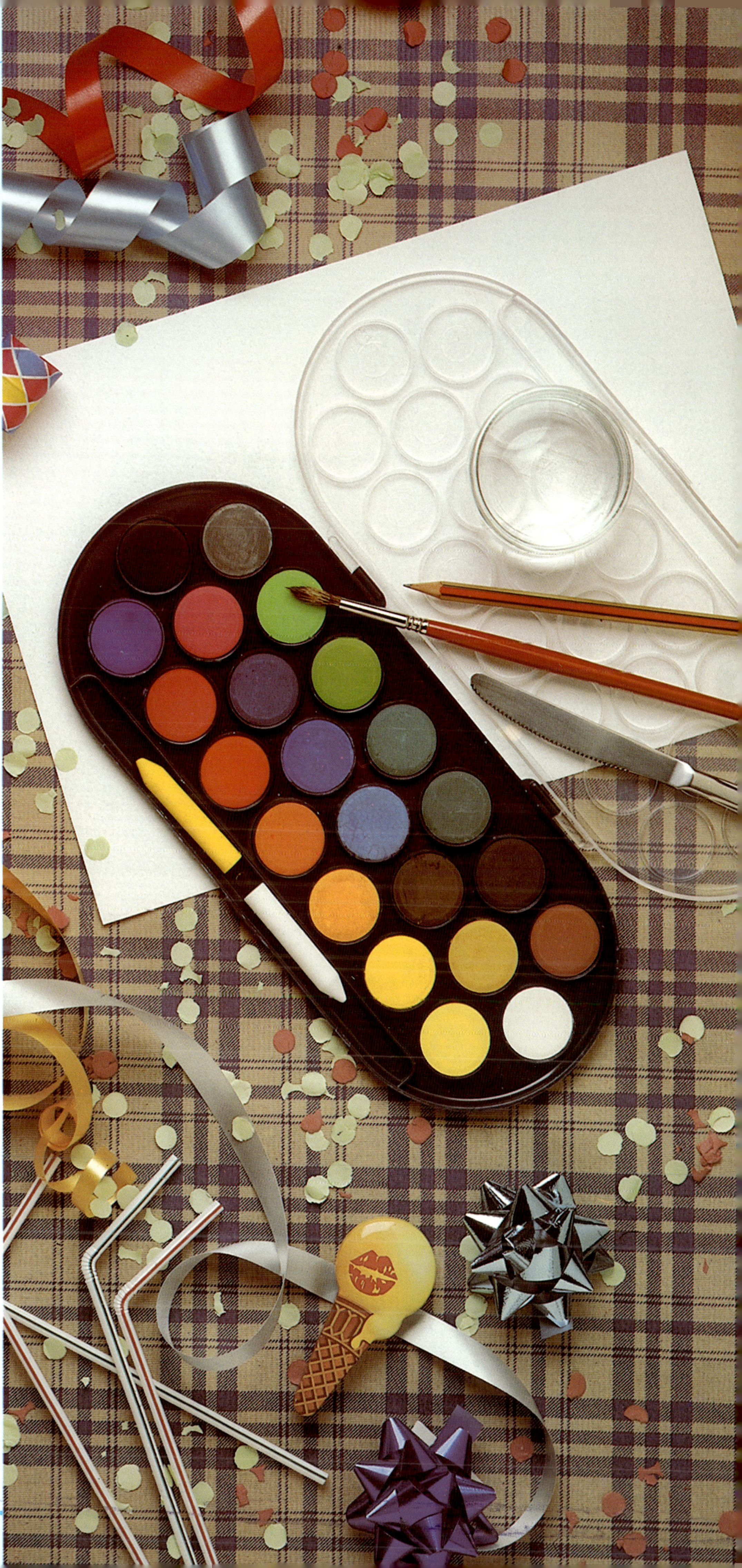

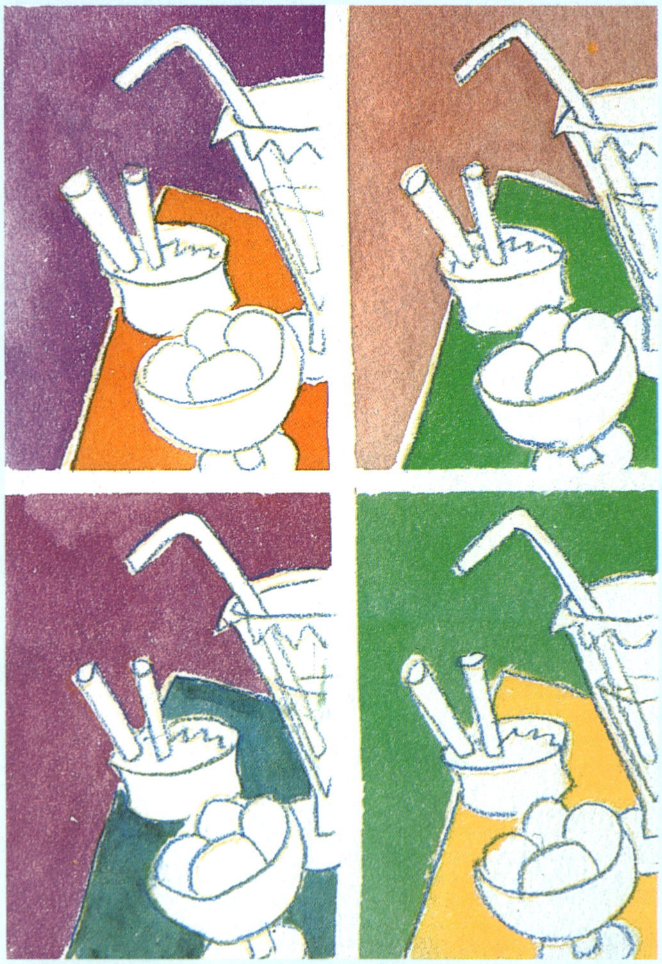

3 Select the watercolors you want for painting the two largest areas: the tablecloth and the background.

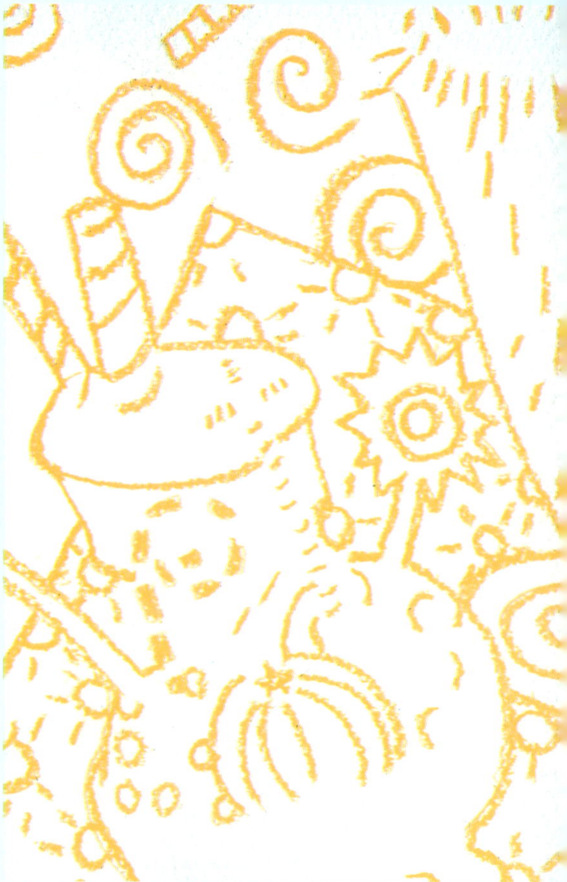

4 With a white wax crayon, decorate the objects and background. Since the crayon lines will be hard to see against the white of the paper, position your drawing so you can see the light reflected from the wax as you draw. In the photograph, we have used a yellow crayon to make the lines visible.

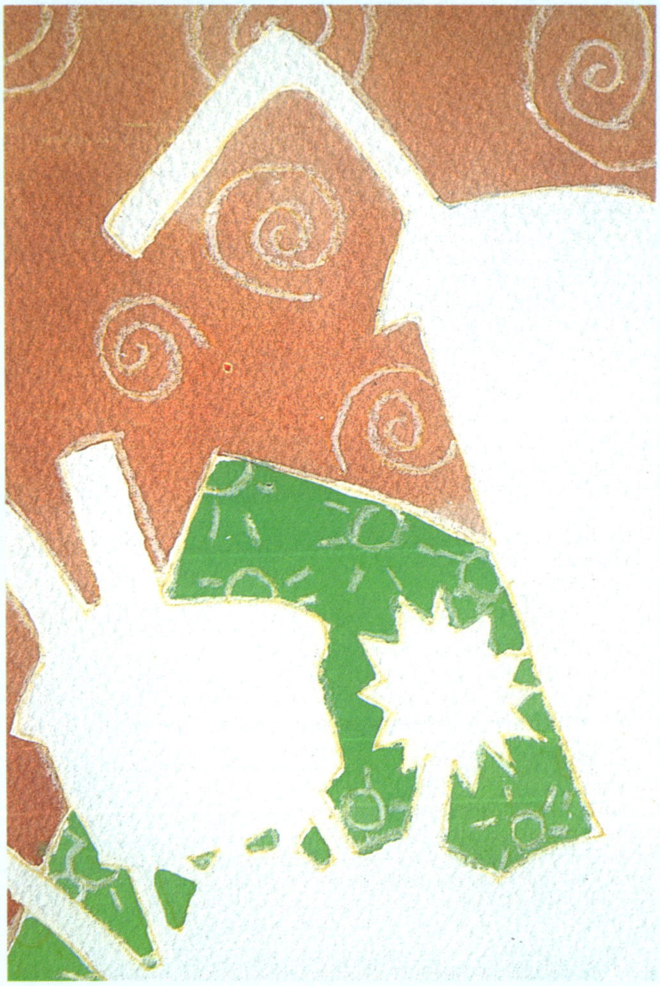

5 Paint the tablecloth and the background with your chosen colors. The patterns you drew with the white crayon will appear. This happens because the wax acts as a barrier that prevents the paper from absorbing the water in the paint.

6 Last, paint the remaining objects using vivid colors.

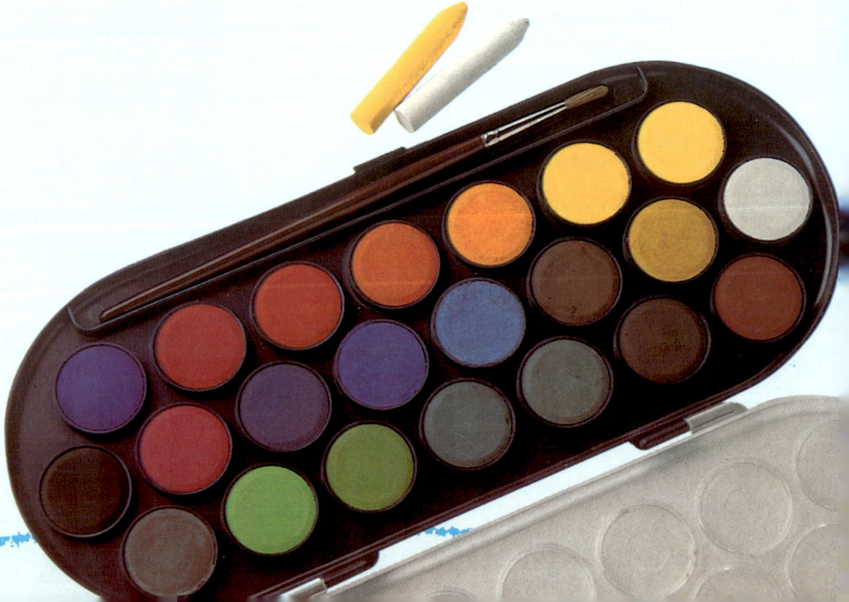

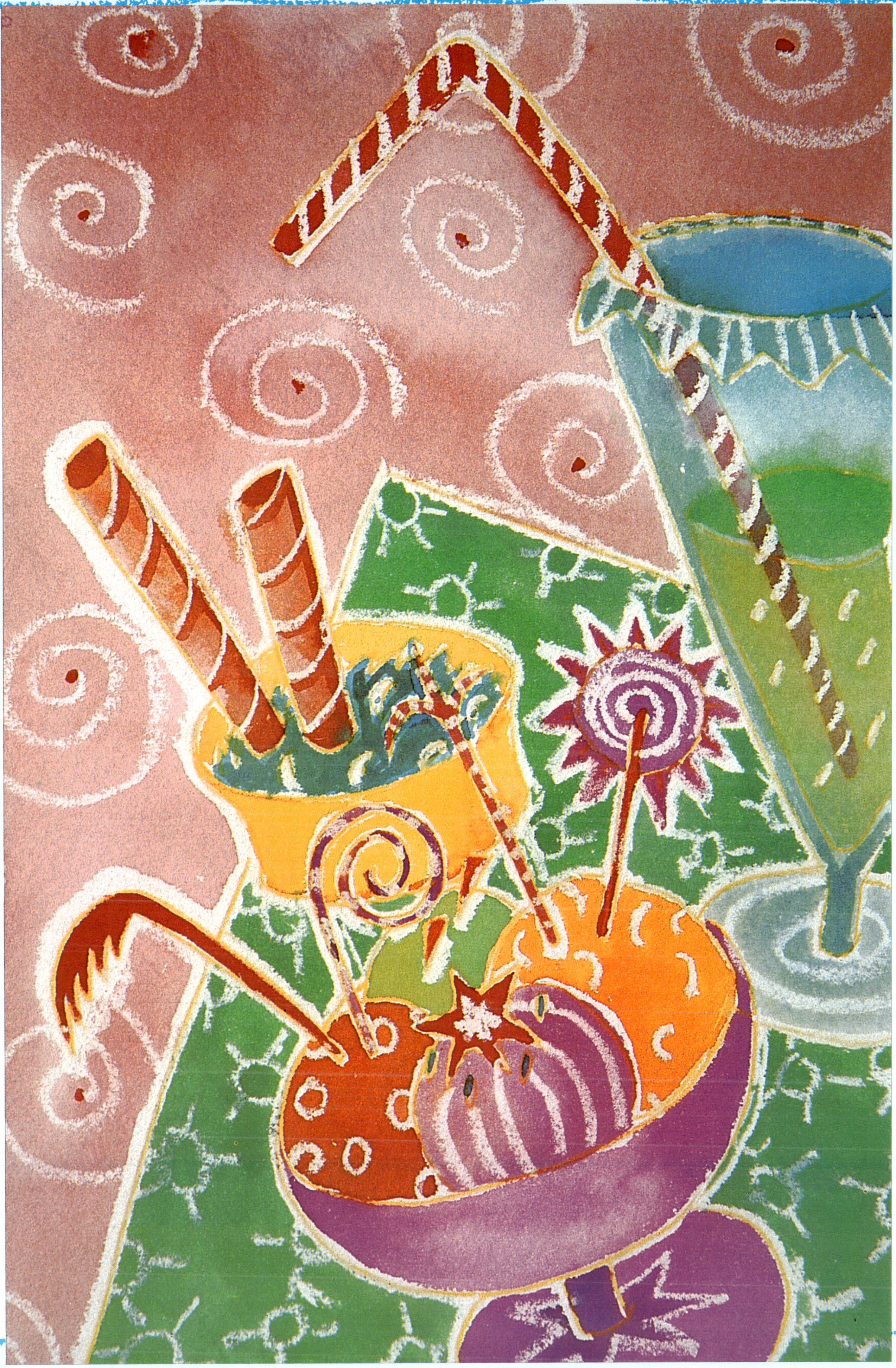

Toys Done with Tissue Paper

The transparency of tissue paper makes it possible to create new colors by gluing one color on top of another.

Use the three-dimensional technique only for the objects. Do the background with flat tissue paper.

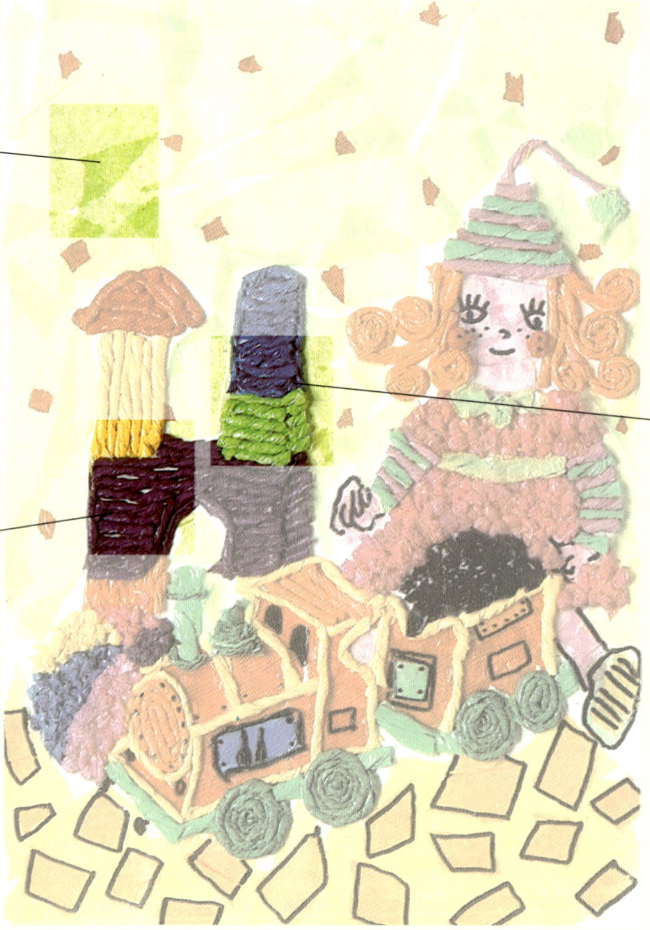

To create a three-dimensional effect, face the strips in one direction on the front surfaces and in a different direction on the side surfaces.

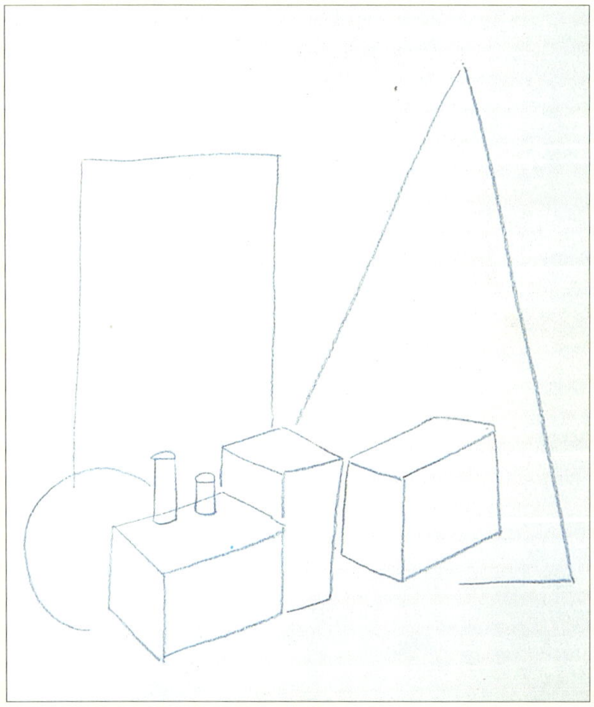

1 Form-sketch each of the objects to find their proportions.

2 Add the details to your drawing.

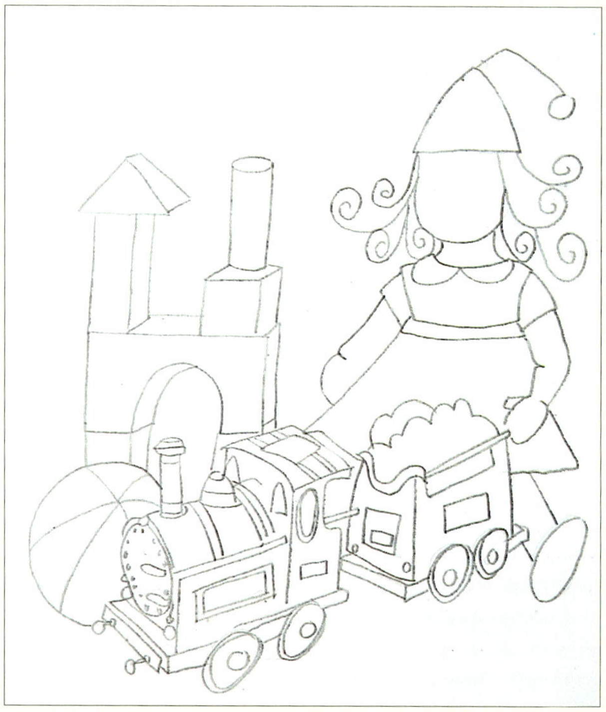

Materials and Techniques

The colors of tissue paper become more intense when a coat of water-thinned white glue is brushed over them.

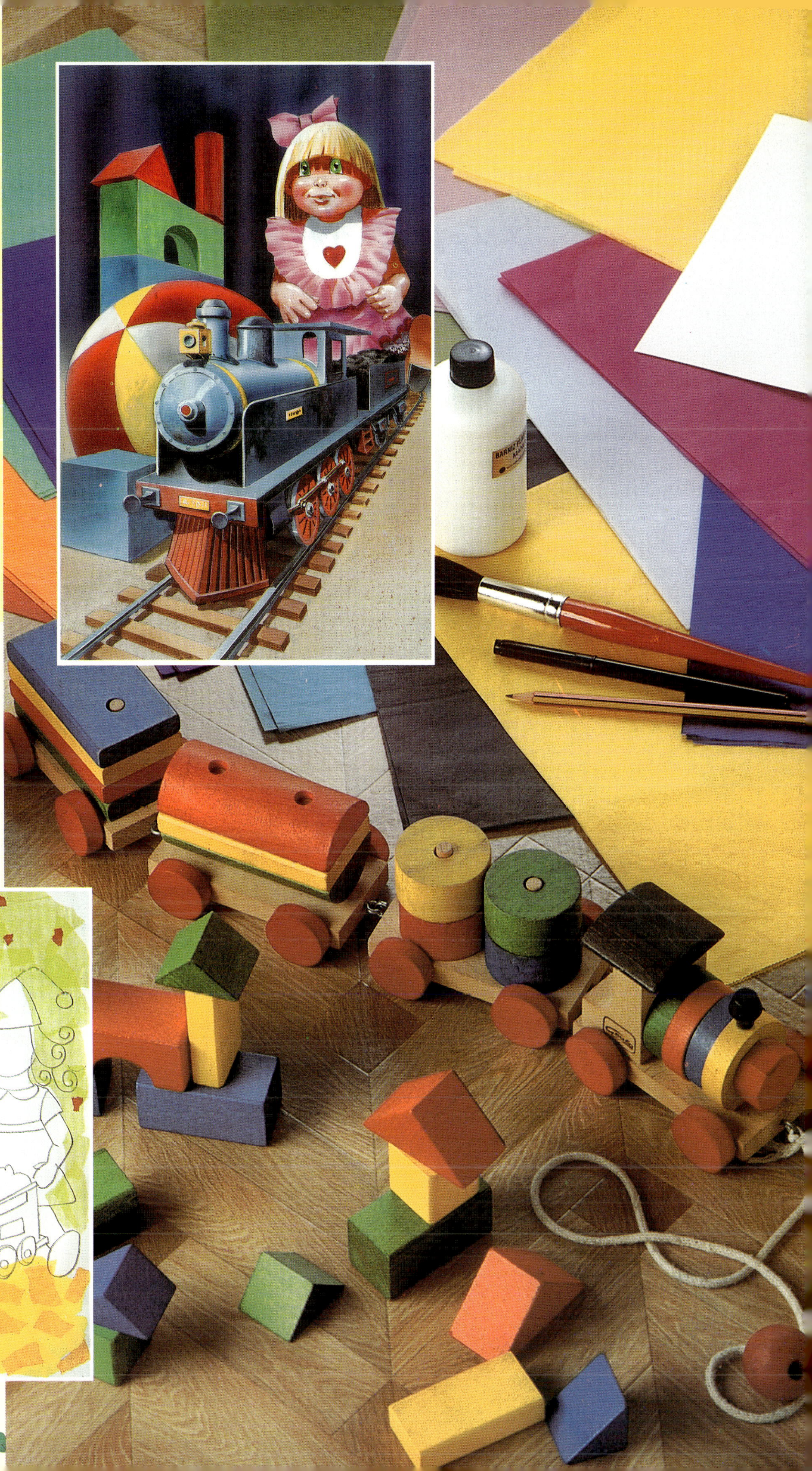

3 With a brush, apply a coat of all-purpose white glue to the background. Then cover it with bits of tissue paper. You can add other colors on top of the first layer.

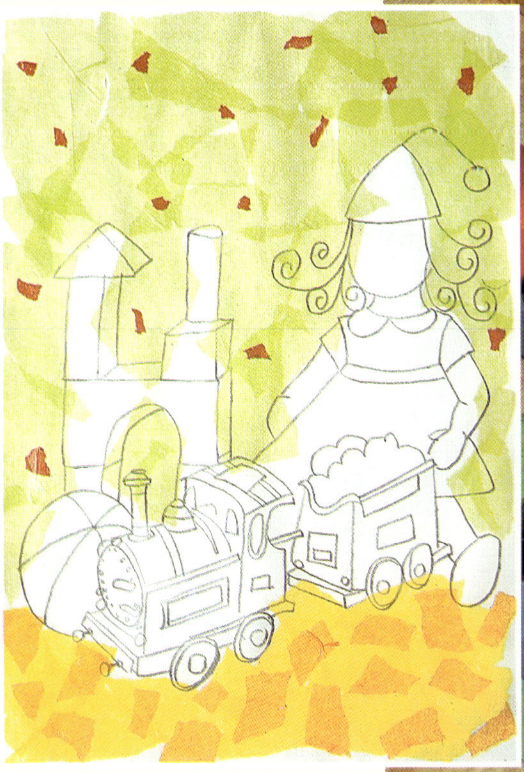

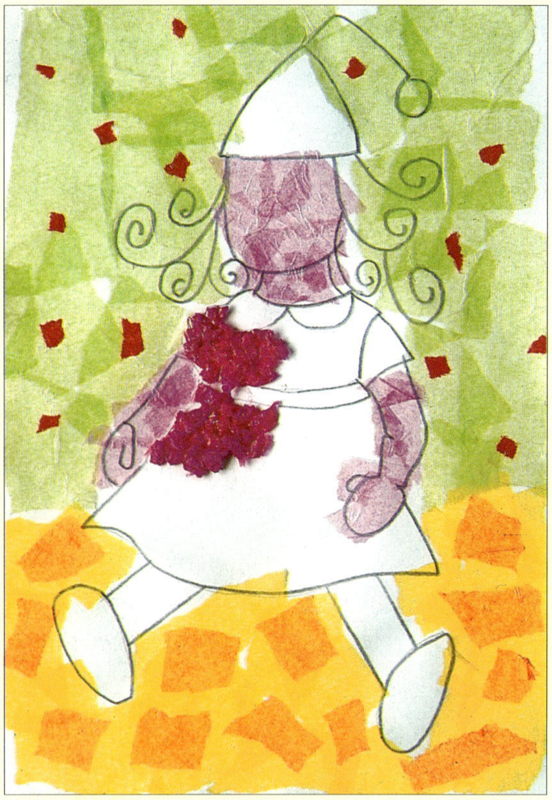

4 To create the toys, first cover the areas you want to leave flat such as the face of the doll. Next, cover the areas where you want volume. You can achieve this effect by gluing small pieces of paper close to one another.

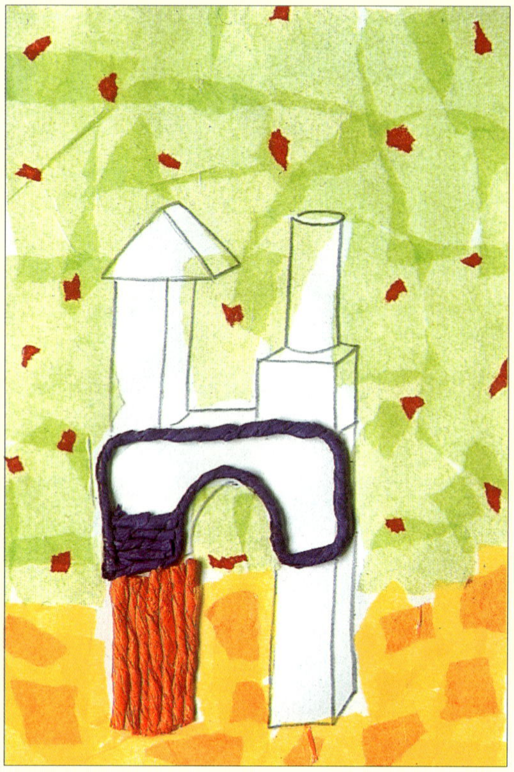

5 You can also crinkle and roll up strips of tissue paper. Then cut the strips into lengths of the appropriate size and paste them on your drawing, one strip alongside the others.

6 For the train wheels, do the same as in the previous step, but make the strips longer; then form coils and glue them in place.

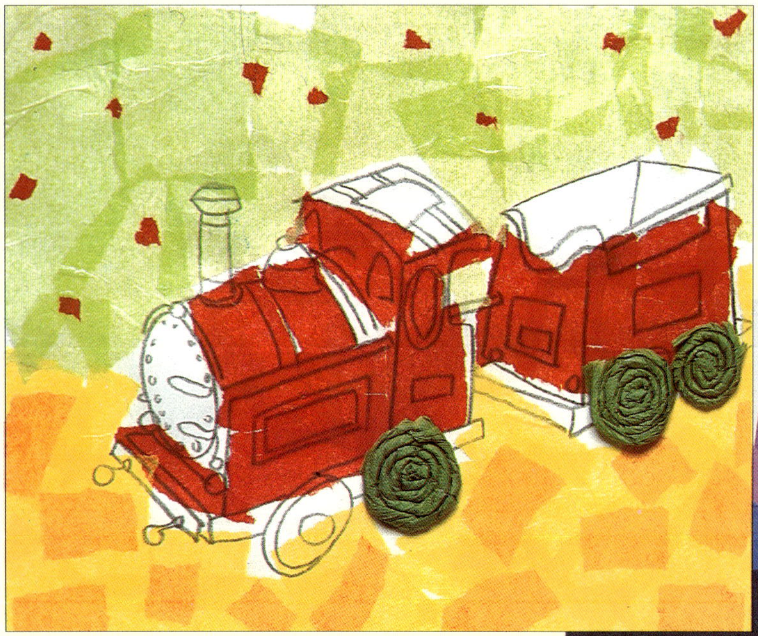

7 Finish by brushing your entire picture with water-thinned white glue. After it dries, touch up some details with a permanent black marker.

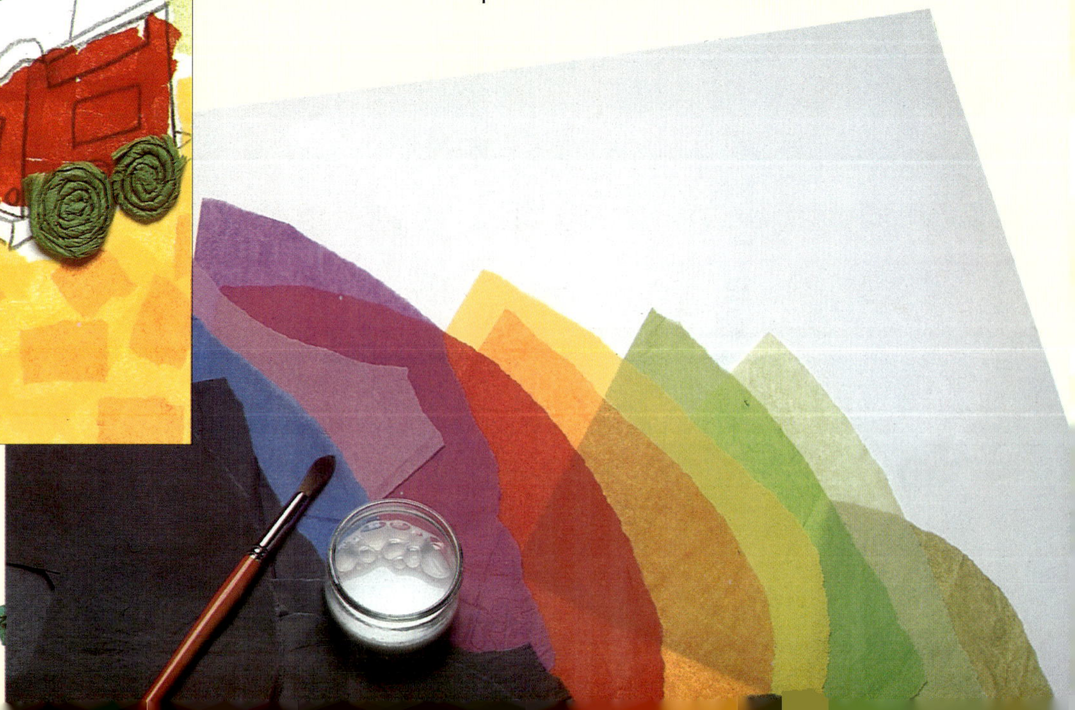

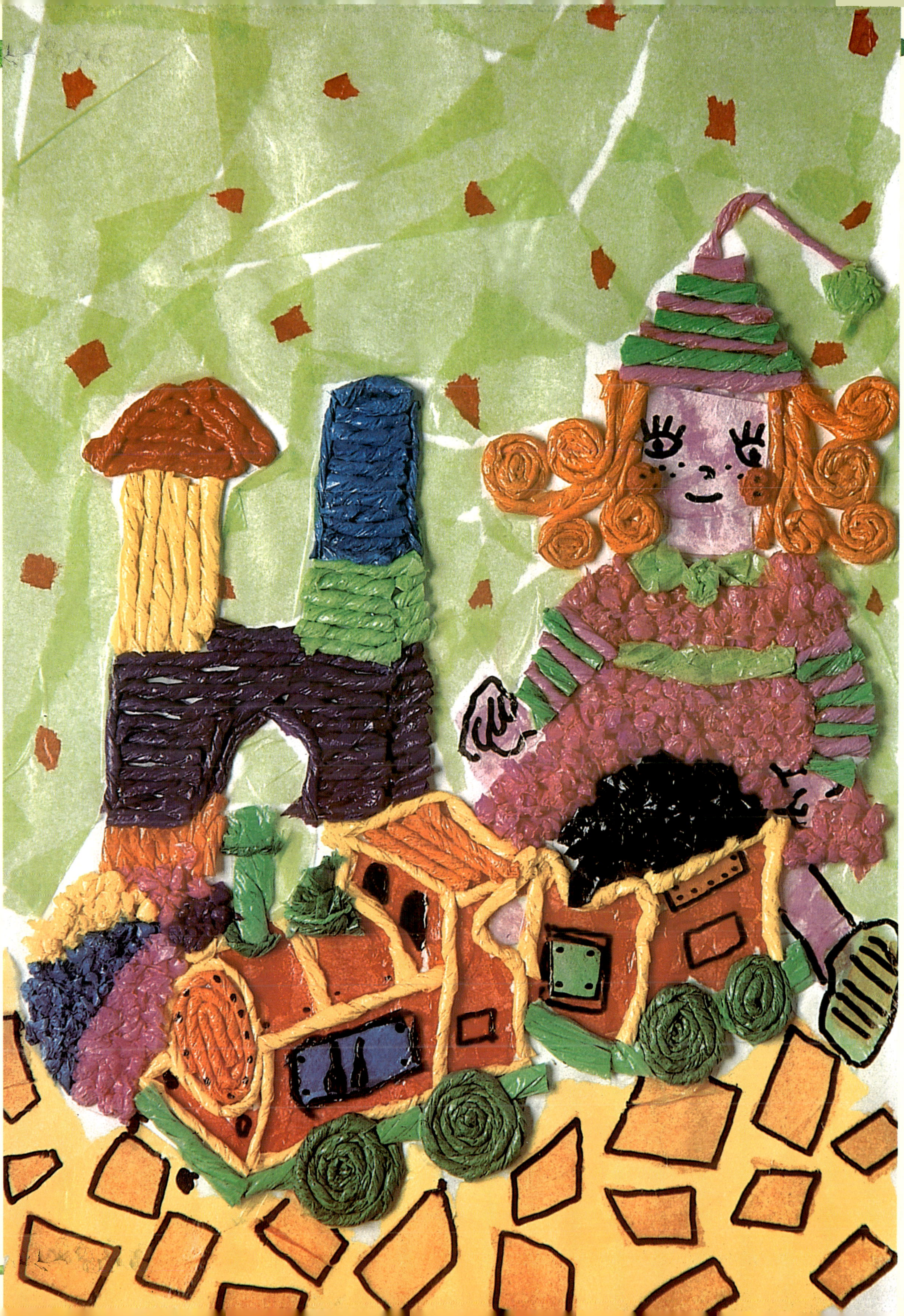

Hiking Equipment with Acetate and Tempera

Vary the patterns of your surfaces to create contrast.

Work the lines using various kinds of tools: the pointed tip of a paint-brush handle, knitting needles, the tips of scissors, and so on.

White stands out best against black, but you can use another color as long as it is visible through the clear *acetate* sheet.

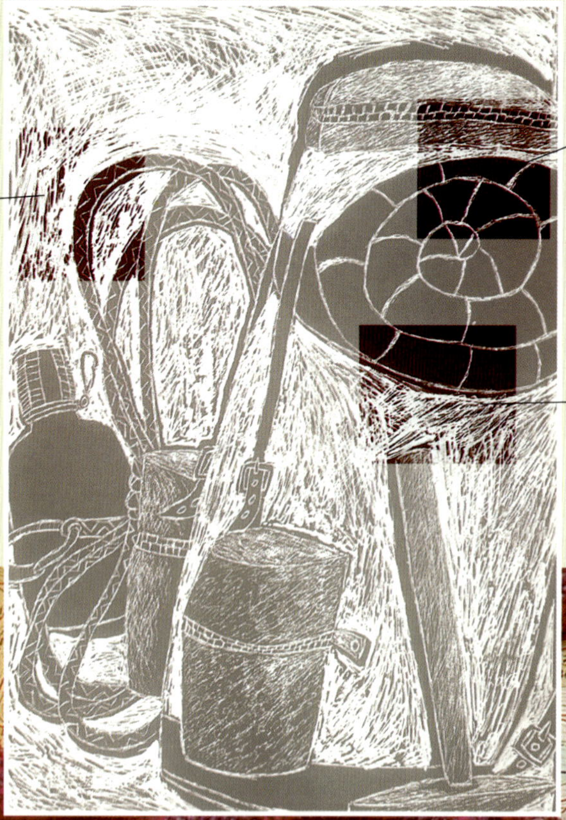

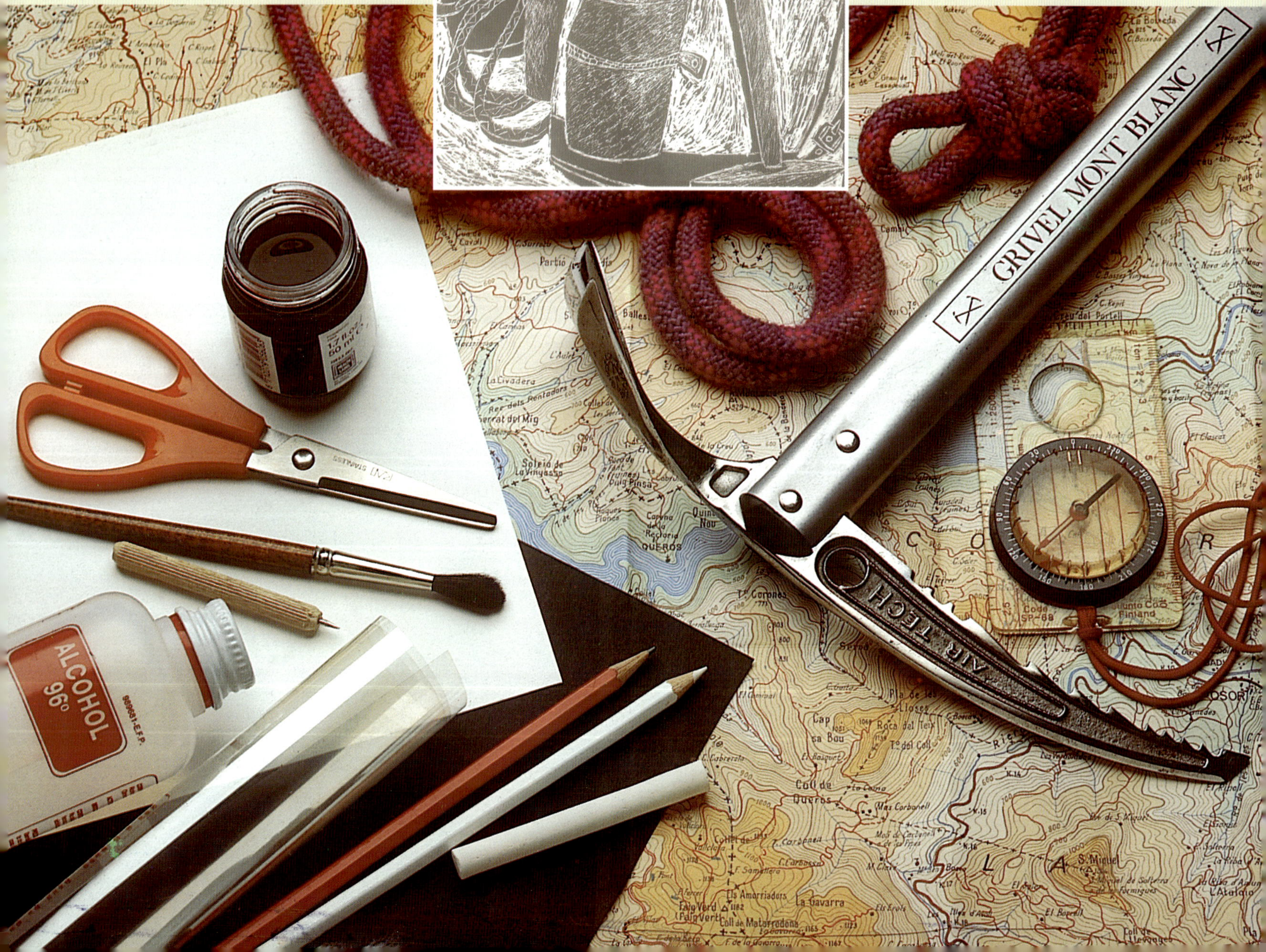

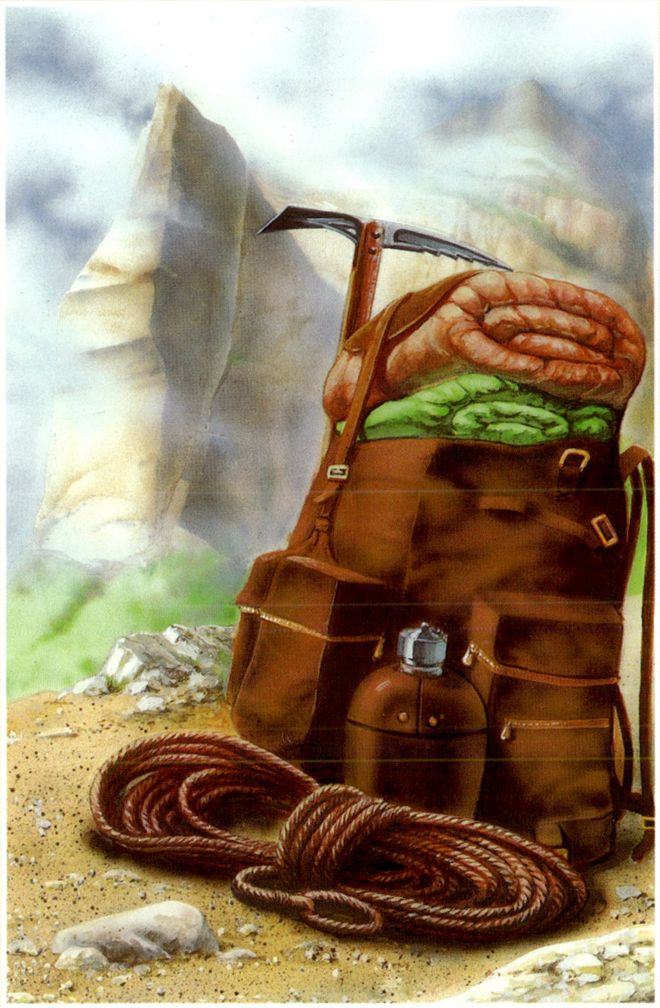

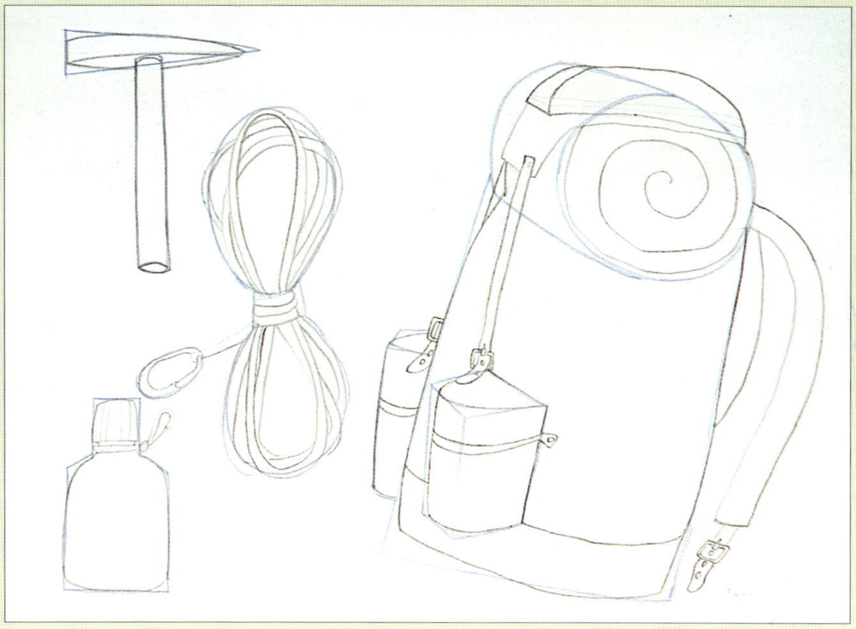

1 To try this technique, we have selected some objects that suggest a hiking theme. First, make the form sketch then the drawing.

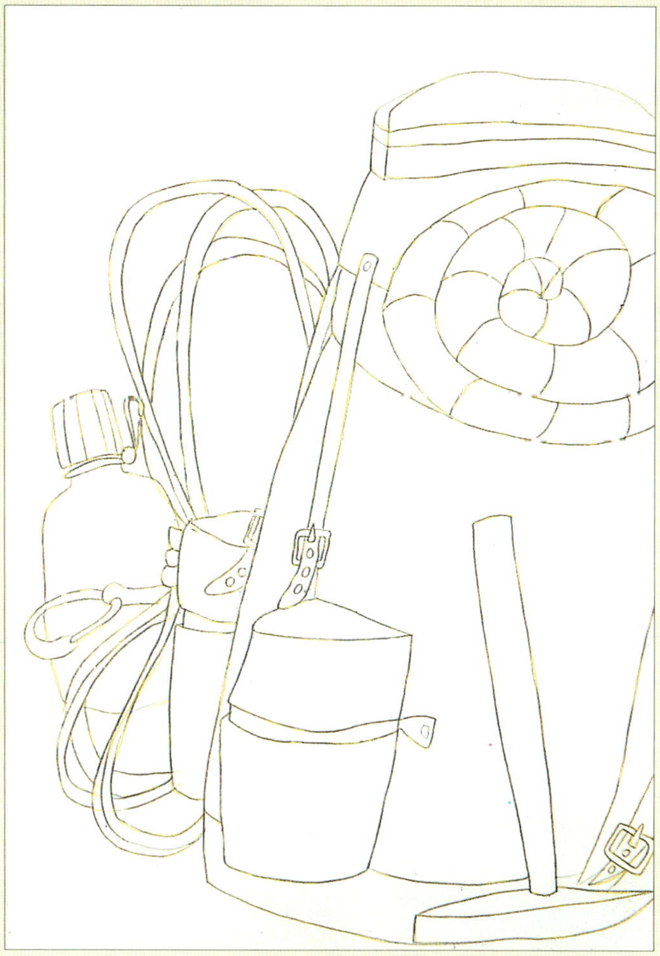

2 Compose your drawing.

Materials and Techniques

For the tempera paint to stick properly to the acetate sheet, the surface must first be cleaned of oily smudges caused by touching the sheet with your fingers. Wipe the surface carefully with a piece of cotton dampened with alcohol (see page 13).